YOUNG PERSON'S
Character
EDUCATION
HAND BOOK

by the EDITORS at JIST

Also in JIST's Young Person's Handbook Series™

Young Person's Occupational Outlook Handbook

JIST Life

Young Person's Character Education Handbook

© 2006 by JIST Publishing, Inc.

Published by JIST Life, an imprint of JIST Publishing, Inc.
8902 Otis Avenue
Indianapolis, IN 46216-1033
Phone: 1-800-648-JIST   Fax: 1-800-JIST-FAX
E-mail: info@jist.com   Web site: www.jist.com

> **Note to educators.** *Young Person's Character Education Handbook* is part of JIST's Young Person's Handbook Series. Related resources include character education and career-related videos, workbooks, assessments, and much more. Call 1-800-648-JIST or visit www.jist.com for more information.
>
> **Quantity discounts are available for JIST products.** Please call 1-800-648-JIST or visit www.jist.com for a free catalog and more information.
>
> **Visit www.jist.com** for information on JIST; book excerpts; and ordering information on our many products. For free information on 14,000 job titles, visit www.careeroink.com.

Acquisitions Editor: Susan Pines
Writer: Nancy Stevenson
Researcher: Earl Boysen
Copy Editor: Chuck Hutchinson
Production Editor: Heather Stith
Cover Illustrator: Chris Sabatino
Interior Illustrator: George McKeon
Interior Designer: Nick Anderson
Cover Designer and Interior Layout: Trudy Coler
Proofreader: Paula Lowell

Printed in the United States of America

10 09 08 07 06 05   9 8 7 6 5 4 3 2 1

Library of Congress Cataloging-in-Publication Data
Young person's character education handbook / by the editors at JIST.
    p. cm. -- (JIST's young person's handbook series)
  Includes index.
  ISBN 1-55864-163-7 (alk. paper)
  1. Moral education--Juvenile literature. 2. Conduct of life--Juvenile literature. I. JIST Life. II. Series.
  LC268.Y68 2006
  370.11'4--dc22   2005021333

ISBN 1-55864-163-7

About This Book

"Do the right thing."

"Treat others the way you want to be treated."

"Tell the truth."

Ever since you were very young, you have heard statements like these. But it is hard to do the right thing all the time. Sometimes you may not know what the right thing is. At other times, you may wonder why doing the right thing is so important.

This handbook helps you with these and similar problems. It describes 50 key "character goals" that many people consider important in school, at home, and in life.

Through examples, checklists, and more, you explore traits and think about how they may affect your life, your future, other people, and the world. You learn how others have made difficult choices related to character. You read suggestions that help you understand and learn to act with character.

This book also reveals many interesting points about character. For example, some traits may be more naturally strong in you than other traits. Traits often work together. Decisions related to character are not always clear and easy.

The introduction gives you more information on how to use the book. We hope the *Young Person's Character Education Handbook* helps you on your journey of character development.

TABLE OF CONTENTS

INTRODUCTION

This book is designed to help you understand and explore a wide variety of character traits. This is important because your character affects your life, other people, and the world in many ways.

Character is about good choices and positive actions. It is about doing the right thing. Character shows itself in your behavior. Character involves your conscience. Character taps into your judgment, your heart, and your thinking. As this book explains, good character can be easy and complex—at the same time!

As you will see, character traits often overlap with personality traits, which are part of who you are. So this book describes traits that may be part of your nature but that also affect your actions. You may be naturally strong in some traits, but all traits described in this book can be learned. That's why we called them "character goals."

This book shows you that character traits work in combination. For example, being honest but insensitive can make you rude. Being generous but not hard working could make you broke.

Also, people do not always act in one way 100 percent of the time. Sometimes people are self-disciplined about one thing, such as practicing the piano. However, they may be less self-disciplined about other things, such as not eating too many desserts.

The important thing is that you think about your actions and try to live in a way that you can respect.

How to Use This Book

This book gives descriptions of 50 important and positive traits in alphabetical order.

You can use this book in many ways. For example, you can

- Read it from beginning to end if you want to be thorough (trait 46).

- Study the traits in any order if you want to be adaptable (trait 2).

- Refer to the book when you have a character-related problem and you want to be inquisitive (trait 29).

If you are using this book in a class, your teacher may assign the material for reading, group discussion, extra credit, homework, or even role-playing.

Information Provided for Each Trait

Each trait in this book follows the same format, so the information is easy to use. Each trait includes these sections:

- *What Does It Mean to Have This Trait?* Definition of the trait. This section helps you understand the trait. You will start thinking about the trait and whether you already have it!

- *This Trait through Time.* Examples of the trait from literature, history, sports, art, science, social studies, or other subjects. This section helps you learn about and look for character in your everyday studies.

- *This Trait in Life.* A case study of the trait from home, school, activities, the community, and other situations. Read about the character-related problems faced by other young people. Read how they solved these problems and what they learned. This section shows character in action.

- *This Trait in Practice.* Suggestions for using the trait and a helpful trait checklist. This section explains how you can try out a trait.

- *Trait Role Models.* Examples of people with this trait. Learn about people with a reputation for having the trait. Some people had disabilities, were poor, had hardships, or faced prejudice. Character helped them become a role model.

- *What's in It for Me?* The effects of having or not having the trait. Learn why developing your character today will bring success in school, at home, and in your future career.

- *Related Words to Explore.* Vocabulary words, including similar traits, synonyms, and antonyms.

An appendix describes Web sites, other books, and videos that will help you learn more about character. Remember that your teachers, counselor, family, and friends can also help you on your character journey!

ACCOUNTABLE

We all take actions in our lives. Some actions are good, and some are bad. When we admit and take responsibility for our actions, it is called being accountable. People who do not admit when they make a mistake are not accountable. They are not willing to accept the consequences of their actions. They may even tell lies to blame others.

People who are accountable often learn from their mistakes. People who do not admit, sometimes even to themselves, that they have made a mistake often do not learn from it. Are you accountable for your actions?

What Does It Mean to Be Accountable?

People take many actions every day and are accountable for these actions. People are accountable for paying bills for items we have bought with a credit card, for example. We are accountable for admitting our mistakes and keeping promises we make to friends.

Who holds us accountable for these things? In some cases, there are laws against certain actions. Not paying a bill may cost a penalty, or worse. Sometimes an organization requires us to be accountable. For example, your school holds you accountable for doing your homework.

In other cases, when we don't keep a promise to a friend, there is probably no law to punish us. Sometimes our conscience holds us accountable. It makes us feel bad when we don't take responsibility for our actions. Though we may find ourselves in complicated situations, being accountable isn't complicated. Being accountable means admitting responsibility for your words or actions.

Young Person's Character Education Handbook, © JIST Life

Accountability through Time

Consider ways in which countries are accountable for their actions:

- Governments are accountable to their citizens to a greater or lesser degree, depending on the country. The United States government has an office of accountability called the Government Accountability Office (GAO). The GAO keeps an eye on the spending habits of the federal government. It is called a watchdog agency because it investigates wrongdoing or errors in government finances. The GAO reports its findings to Congress. As a result of misbehavior within the government, Congress may take action or even change laws.

- All the countries in the world play a part in maintaining our environment. Keeping air and water clean and healthy is a responsibility we all share. Every country's actions can have an impact on our environment. Some countries sign agreements to make changes in their behavior to help the environment. Whether or not they formally agree, countries should be accountable for the actions of their citizens, businesses, and lawmakers regarding the environment.

Countries, individuals, and organizations take many actions for which there are no rules. Being accountable for actions, even if nobody is forcing you to be, is a sign of good character and maturity.

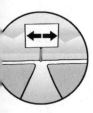

Being Accountable in Life

Consider this situation:

John moved to the Phoenix area mid-year. He started as a student at Jefferson Middle School a few days ago. The student body president came by John's class on Tuesday to take a vote on five items before the student council. Because John didn't know anything about the issues, he did not vote. But he noticed that everybody else in the class voted yes on all five issues, which seemed odd.

The next day, John stopped the student body president, Serena, in the cafeteria and asked about the vote. "Yeah," she replied, "Kids at this school don't seem to feel accountable for what goes on in the school government. They don't care enough to study the issues. But when there's a problem, they all blame the student council."

Do the students in your school feel accountable for the things that go on there? Are you accountable to learn about school issues and vote in an informed way? If you don't learn about issues and vote what you feel, are you accountable for the results?

> **"**What people say, what people do, and what they say they do are entirely different things.**"**
> —Margaret Mead, Anthropologist

Being Accountable in Practice

The next time you make a mistake, think about how to be accountable for it. Is there somebody you should admit your mistake to? Is there something you should do to make up for the mistake? Do you deserve some kind of punishment? And are you willing to go through that punishment?

Now consider the consequences if you pretended not to have made the mistake. How would you feel? Is it possible somebody else will be blamed for your mistake? Consider the worst thing that somebody will do to you if you admit your mistake. Would it be so bad? Would admitting your mistake be worthwhile to feel better about what you did? If what happened was an accident or honest mistake, should you still be accountable?

ACCOUNTABILITY CHECKLIST

◯ Admit when you make a mistake.

◯ Never put the blame on others if your actions cause a problem.

◯ If you say you will do something, do it. If you can't do it for some reason, take responsibility for your inaction.

◯ If you are responsible for money, honestly account for how you spend it.

◯ If you are responsible for the actions of others—pets, for example— be responsible for problems they cause.

◯ If there is no rule or law to hold you accountable, decide what to do based on your conscience.

Accountable Role Models

Here are some people in government roles. Each has shown account-ability in complex situations.

- Janet Reno was the first female Attorney General of the United States. Around the time she took office, the FBI was negotiating with a religious cult called the Branch Davidians in Waco, Texas. There were reports that these people had illegal weapons and were abusing children in their care. A month after she took office, Reno approved a plan, with the agreement of the President, to storm the buildings. Fires broke out, and most of the people inside the buildings were killed. Although the situation had begun before she took office, and the President had approved her action, Reno had approved the plan. She held herself accountable for the disaster and offered her resignation. The President did not accept it. She continued in her job.

- In 1990, President George H.W. Bush signed the first letter of apology to the Japanese-Americans who were placed in internment camps during World War II. The letter and cash payments were presented to survivors of the experience. Many view putting people in these camps as a violation of human rights. Others claimed it was necessary to keep the country safe from spies during the war with Japan. Many consider the letter to be too little, too late. But it is an example of a government being accountable for its actions.

What's in It for Me?

Consider these real-life consequences of being accountable:

- People who are not accountable are rarely given responsibility in their lives or their work.

- Accountable people recognize and admit when they make mistakes and thereby often learn from them.

- People who are accountable are put in positions of trust. These positions often pay more money and earn more fame and respect.

Related Words to Explore

Here are some words related to the trait of being accountable and to its opposite:

- Answerable
- Responsible
- Liable
- Owning up to
- Direct

- Evasive
- Shifty
- Vague
- Elusive

ADAPTABLE

Change is something that happens all the time in life. Perhaps you will change schools, move to a new town, or join a new club at school. Each change means that you have to adjust to the way other people behave.

Being able to adapt, or change your behavior to match new people or situations, can be important to your success in life. How adaptable are you?

What Does It Mean to Be Adaptable?

The variety of customs, ideas, and behaviors is a wonderful thing about our world. Being adaptable means that you are able to change your behavior to fit a new situation or new information. This does not mean that you act dishonestly or pretend to change your personality to make other people happy. It means that you use the latest information to act appropriately in response.

Adapting may mean learning new ways to explain your ideas or beliefs to other people. For example, if you visit Japan, a friend may explain that in Japan it is not appropriate to express too much pride. Knowing this, you do not boast about your family or your accomplishments.

We live our lives in situations, places, and groups that change how we behave to get along with others.

Adaptability through Time

You see adaptability in many areas of life. Here are some examples:

- In biology, adaptability has helped whole species to survive. Think about your body's ability to adapt to very cold weather and very warm weather. When you are sick and get a mild fever, your body may be adapting to an infection. Your body's immune system works better at higher temperatures to fight off germs. People who live in very cold temperatures all the time, such as the Eskimo population, tend to have more body fat to keep them warm. These adaptive measures in nature help life to survive.

- In the world of art, change and adaptability are constant. An artist may produce something strange and unusual today, but people learn to like the new style and forget the old style. In 1913, Igor Stravinsky wrote a piece of music called *The Rite of Spring*. It was so different from the current style of music that a riot broke out when it was first performed. Today, we consider it a great piece of music. Consider how rap music introduced a new style. How have people adapted to this music? How will it be looked at 20 years from now?

When you look at fashions or ideas, consider how your own tastes or ideas change over time. How did you dress three years ago? If you moved to a country where your style of dress was offensive, what would you do? If all your classmates changed their style of dress and you didn't, would that be okay?

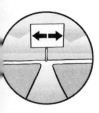

Being Adaptable in Life

Consider this situation:

Tasha and her sister Olivia are very different. Tasha is a free spirit who goes her own way. Olivia pays more attention to the rules and fits in well with everybody.

When their parents announced they were moving, Tasha was miserable, but Olivia looked forward to the change. At their new school, they found out that if they were late for class, they had to go to the principal's office. In their old school, things were not so strict.

Tasha had a hard time adapting and was often late for class. She spent a lot of time in the principal's office. Olivia adapted to the rules and was on time to class. She joined new groups and got along with her new classmates. Tasha spent a lot of time alone.

One afternoon Tasha and Olivia had a fight. "You're just a wimp, trying to impress the teachers," said Tasha. "Well, you spend part of every day in the principal's office, while I get to hang out at the mall," said Olivia.

Who is right? Has Olivia given in to pressure or has she adapted to a new situation? Is Tasha showing courage by staying true to herself? Or is she wasting her time and energy sticking with old ways of doing things?

> **"***If one does not know to which port one is sailing, no wind is favorable.***"**
>
> —Seneca, Dramatist, Philosopher, and Politician

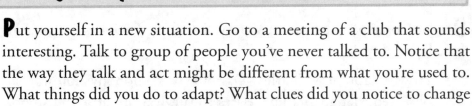

Being Adaptable in Practice

Put yourself in a new situation. Go to a meeting of a club that sounds interesting. Talk to group of people you've never talked to. Notice that the way they talk and act might be different from what you're used to. What things did you do to adapt? What clues did you notice to change your behavior to be more in tune with the new group?

Fitting in with a new group may or may not work. You may find that some groups are not right for you. In that case, you can respect their beliefs but decide not to be part of those groups and not to adapt your style to theirs. If you decide not to adapt in the long term and find another place or group where you fit, it's okay. However, if you want to or have to be part of a group, adapting might be a healthy way to deal with change.

ADAPTABILITY CHECKLIST

- ⬭ Listen to others to see how they are different before making judgments about how you might adapt.
- ⬭ Decide what changes are comfortable for you.
- ⬭ Don't lie or pretend if a change makes you uncomfortable.
- ⬭ Look for things you have in common with the new group or situation.
- ⬭ Determine whether adapting makes sense in the long run.
- ⬭ Change your behavior to fit the most current information you have.

Adaptable Role Models

Here are some people from various walks of life. Each has a reputation for adaptability.

- How adaptable Charles Darwin was, nobody knows. He observed that adaptation relates to survival in nature. His book, *The Origin of the Species*, presented the theory that people evolved over time from lower life forms by adapting to climate and other factors. His theory caused a strong reaction among people who could not easily adapt their thinking to this new idea.

- Helen Keller was 19 months old when she fell ill with a fever. When she recovered, she was deaf and blind. Her family did not know how to cope with the situation. When Helen was six, they brought in a private teacher named Annie Sullivan. Sullivan challenged all the behavior that young Helen had learned in her short life. She fought to teach her ways to communicate and behave. Helen not only adapted to survive, but she became an author and teacher herself. Keller's triumph can inspire us when we face change.

- Anne Frank was a rebellious girl when her family went into hiding from the Nazis in World War II. She was forced to live in an attic with many others and to give up many things. Anne fought some things but adapted to others, in great part by writing her thoughts in a diary. Her father found and published that diary after the war—after Anne had died in a concentration camp. Her diary inspires anyone who must find a way to rise above change.

What's in It for Me?

Consider these real-life consequences of being adaptable:

- People who cannot adapt to new circumstances are rarely happy because they never fit in and rarely get ahead.

- Adaptable people are good at adjusting to changes in circumstances. They receive promotions at work and are recognized for being flexible.

- People who cannot adapt are often left behind when change comes. They may go off and find another situation that is similar to what they are used to. However, some day even that situation may disappear.

Related Words to Explore

Here are some words related to the trait of being adaptable and to its opposite:

- Flexible
- Accommodating
- Adjustable
- Conforming

- Changeable
- Inflexible
- Rigid
- Unaccommodating

> **"**Everyone thinks of changing the world, but no one thinks of changing himself. **"**
> —Leo Tolstoy, Novelist

ALTRUISTIC

Being altruistic means caring about the welfare of other people with-out expecting anything in return. Sometimes we care for others to get a reward or to make them love us. An altruistic person is unselfish and finds that caring for others can be its own reward.

Are you an altruistic person?

What Does It Mean to Be Altruistic?

A friend helps a friend because she wants to grow and keep the friend-ship. A man gives a donation to a charity so others will think good things about him. A nurse cares for others for a paycheck and for job satisfaction. All of these acts are kind and caring, but they may not be altruistic.

In an altruistic act, you don't do something for recog-nition or reward. If you help a stranger and never tell anybody what you did or expect to see that person again, you are altruistic. If you mail a donation to a charity but don't give your name or expect to be thanked, you are altruistic.

Because you often get some reward from any kind act you do, it is hard to see any act as purely altruistic. But consider the motives for your acts in trying to figure out whether you are acting altruistically.

Altruism through Time

Altruism is often seen in extreme circumstances. Natural disasters or times of war can bring out altruism. Consider these examples from history and literature:

- The December 2004 tsunami (an earthquake and resulting tidal wave) that centered in Indonesia took thousands of lives. People from all over the world sent money. Doctors worked to help the injured. Others came to rebuild homes and roads. Some people were paid to help. Others paid their own way to work with victims. Many people had to sacrifice time, money, and more to help. Expecting no formal recognition, many people showed great altruism. Would you leave your home to work in hard conditions to help somebody you never met?

- Charles Dickens' novel *A Tale of Two Cities* takes place during the French Revolution. In it, Dickens wrote about a character who had lived an irresponsible and selfish life. At the end of the book, this character willingly takes the place of another man who is sentenced to die to save the other man's life. At the execution, he says, "Tis a far, far better thing I do than I have ever done before." By dying in the other man's place, he finally performs an altruistic act for which there can be no reward.

Why is an altruistic act finer than others? Is it possible, or even desirable, to be altruistic all the time?

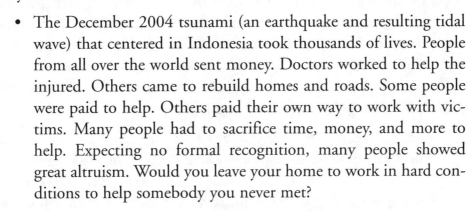

> **"** Real generosity is doing something nice for someone who will never find out. **"**
> —Frank A. Clark, Writer

Being Altruistic in Life

Consider this situation:

> *Ellen Hathaway had begun substitute teaching in her town. On her second day, she was asked to teach an art class. During class, students made a mess with paints and other materials. Although Ellen asked them to clean up their own spaces before the end of class, most students did not. With only a 15-minute break before her next class, Ellen began to clean up herself. She was upset that the students took advantage of her substitute status to disobey her.*
>
> *After a minute, there was a knock at the classroom door. It was Tamika, one of the students who had cleaned up her desk before leaving. "Ms. Hathaway, can I help?" Ellen knew that Tamika was giving up part of her lunch break to help. Because Ellen was a substitute teacher, she couldn't do anything for Tamika, such as give her a better grade or nominate her for an award. As Ellen and Tamika finished up, Ellen thanked her. "No problem," said Tamika, who hurried to the lunchroom to grab a sandwich before her next class. Tamika's friend asked her why she was late, and Tamika just smiled.*

Why did Tamika help Ellen Hathaway? There was no reward in it for her. She missed part of her lunch break to help. She never told anybody what she did. Would you have done the same just to help somebody with no thought of reward?

> **❝** The greatest pleasure I know is to do a good action by stealth, and to have it found out by accident. **❞**
> —Charles Lamb, Essayist

Being Altruistic in Practice

The next time you see somebody who needs help, don't stop to think about whether you have time to help or whether that person might reward you for helping. Help first, and then consider the pros and cons of your actions later.

After you have helped the person, list the pros and cons of your actions. Ask yourself how often you stop yourself from getting involved or helping somebody because it's inconvenient. Consider whether it's sometimes wise to avoid helping somebody. Why? Could some people misunderstand your actions? Could the cost of helping sometimes be too high? Could you help people without reward more often?

ALTRUISM CHECKLIST

- ◯ Offer help without expecting or accepting a reward.

- ◯ Show concern for people you don't know, realizing that you may never see them again.

- ◯ The next time you help somebody, don't tell anyone about what you did.

- ◯ Make the act of helping more important than the cost or reward to you. Be willing to give up time, money, or effort without reward.

Altruistic Role Models

Here are some people who have a reputation for being altruistic.

- Florence Nightingale was a nurse during the Crimean War in the 1800s. During the war, many British soldiers were dying from disease and wounds. A commission sent a group of nurses to Turkey. This group was led by Florence Nightingale. Her night rounds by lamp light earned her the name of Lady of the Lamp because she was tireless in caring for the sick. Her efforts not only saved many lives, but helped to raise nursing to a respectable position in society. Nightingale was so disinterested in fame or reward that she returned home under an assumed name and refused photographs or interviews all her life.

- Harriet Tubman was born into slavery in the American South. As a teenager she tried to protect another field worker from a beating. The overseer swung at the worker and hit Tubman in the head, causing an injury that gave her pain the rest of her life. After escaping herself, she helped more than 300 other slaves to move along the Underground Railroad to safety. During her life, she made 19 trips back to the South to help others. In doing so, she was in danger of being caught and returned to slavery.

- Dr. Albert Schweitzer was a French missionary and surgeon. In 1952, he won the Nobel Peace Prize. Earlier in his life, he was a minister and an accomplished musician. When he decided to go to Africa as a missionary, he put himself through medical school to become a doctor. He worked in French Equatorial Africa, building a hospital to offer health care to natives. With the Nobel Peace Prize money, he started a hospital for people with leprosy, a disfiguring disease.

What's in It for Me?

Altruistic people don't ask what's in it for them, so this one is tricky! However, altruistic people often

- Earn the respect of others.

- Have high self-esteem because they feel good about what they do.

- Feel less stress because they don't expect others to notice what they do, so they don't worry about getting rewards or recognition.

Related Words to Explore

Here are some words related to the trait of being altruistic and to its opposite:

- Caring
- Sacrificing
- Helpful
- Kind

- Concerned
- Unselfish
- Selfish
- Self-serving

> **❝**You have not lived a perfect day, even though you have earned your money, unless you have done something for someone who cannot repay you.**❞**
> —**Ruth Smeltzer**

AMBITIOUS

Ambitious people want to be successful. Success can be defined in different ways: money, power, fame, or achievement, for example. Most ambitious people are good at setting goals and reaching them. They don't let setbacks stop them.

In what ways are you ambitious?

What Does It Mean to Be Ambitious?

Ambition is simply the desire for success. It can help you achieve great things. But ambition is sometimes combined with negative traits such as greed or ruthlessness. There is nothing wrong with wanting to be successful. However, the way you achieve your ambitions and treat people in the process is important.

Ambition, used well, can help you stick with something, work hard, focus on a goal, and reach it. Ambition misused can make you unfeeling toward other people who get in the way of your success.

Ambition helps people succeed in their careers, so many famous people have this trait. Politicians, famous entertainers, successful business people, and others often want the fame and power that come with success. That drive helps them achieve great things and build great things with lasting value for the world.

What are you ambitious for?

Ambition through Time

You see examples of ambition in history, for example:

- The Panama Canal was built so that ships would not have to travel around the tip of South America to go from the Atlantic to the Pacific. Building the canal took many years. In the 1800s, a French team headed by Ferdinand de Lesseps began exploring the isthmus of Panama. Though the French team began building the canal, in the end they failed. The Americans took over under Theodore Roosevelt as president. He saw the canal as a way to increase both economic and political power for the United States. His drive and ambition were key to the successful completion of the canal.

- The Roman Empire took over a great deal of Europe in its time. Driven by personal ambition, Julius Caesar led Roman armies to conquer others. But the Empire also spread benefits such as a road system and aqueducts for irrigation. Both personal and national ambition drove one of the greatest expansions in history.

Without ambition, many dreams would be left unrealized. Even though ambitious people may have their own success most in mind, their drive causes great things to happen that may benefit us all.

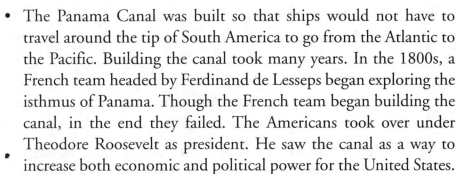

"A man with ambition and love for his blessings here on earth is ever so alive."
—**Pearl Bailey, Entertainer**

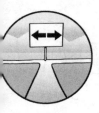

Being Ambitious in Life

Consider this situation:

Kailyn always seemed to be on the move. During the school band candy sale, she sold twice as much candy as anybody else. For her efforts, she won the top seller prize. She wanted to go into her father's business after leaving school. He told her math was important in business, so she was always the best in her math class. She earned A's every semester.

When one of the kids in Kailyn's class was in an accident and her family needed help with medical bills, the principal challenged the class to find a way to help. Kailyn stepped forward and said she'd take on the project. She set a goal to raise $10,000 in two months. Her parents warned her that this goal seemed like too much to do.

In two months, Kailyn organized bake sales and car washes. She herself worked long hours making phone calls to kids' parents and getting the local newspaper to publish articles about their efforts. At the end of two months, Kailyn's classmates had raised $14,300 for the boy's family.

Ambition can help you gain personal success or succeed in helping others. If you want success, you should develop ambition that helps you focus on a goal and keep after it. But always remember to choose your goals wisely.

Being Ambitious in Practice

Think about the areas of your life in which success is important. Do you want to be successful at school, at work, or at a hobby? Do you want to become a successful musician or writer? Find a kind of success that is important to you, and focus your energies on achieving it.

AMBITION CHECKLIST

- Have a clear goal.
- Decide what success means for you.
- Don't let setbacks stop you from reaching your goal.
- Consider how you will treat people who get in the way of your goal. Keep a balance between ambition and respect for others.
- Enjoy your success when it comes, but don't use your success to hurt others.

"Keep away from people who try to belittle your ambitions. Small people always do that, but the really great make you feel that you, too, can become great.**"**
—Mark Twain, Writer

Ambitious Role Models

Here are people with a reputation for being ambitious.

- Indira Gandhi was the daughter of the first Prime Minister of India, Jawaharial Nehru. She was a brilliant strategist who sought political power. The people in the cabinets that served her were often considered weak, which let her exercise her own power. She led India to become self-sufficient in food production and created successful environmental protection policies. At one point when opponents tried to remove her, she found an article in the constitution granting her extreme powers in a state of emergency.

- Donald Trump started working with his father in his construction business in Brooklyn. From there, he entered the New York City real estate market, making millions from smart deals. Today, some of the impressive buildings in New York are named "Trump," such as The Trump Palace and Trump Plaza. His personal wealth is estimated at $1.4 billion, though Trump claims it is more than $3 billion.

Ambition can build great buildings, provide jobs for many people, or lead a country to growth and development. Ambitious people find a way to succeed, though ambition also sometimes requires sacrifice. What is success worth to you?

> **"**Ambition is putting a ladder against the sky.**"**
> **—American Proverb**

What's in It for Me?

Consider these real-life consequences of being ambitious:

- Ambitious people can achieve great things.

- Ambitious people often reach success in the world and may gain money and fame.

- People may admire ambitious people because of their focus and enthusiasm.

- Ambitious people are often put in charge of projects because of their drive.

Related Words to Explore

Here are some words related to the trait of being ambitious and to its opposite:

- Determined
- Go-getting
- Striving
- Motivated

- Visionary
- Unambitious
- Lazy
- Unmotivated

BOLD

The dictionary uses words such as *courageous* and *adventurous* to describe the meaning of bold. This combination of bravery and the willingness to do something new and different, perhaps even startling, is what makes someone bold.

Bold people are not just brave; they strike out in new directions. They are willing to take chances or do things differently than they have been done before. Are you a bold person?

What Does It Mean to Be Bold?

Some people are brave and do things that might scare others. Some people are inventive and come up with new ways of doing things. But some people combine bravery with inventiveness. They strike out in new directions even though doing so may be frightening. Bold people show a unique style. They gain the admiration of others because they are willing to try something new.

Bold people tend not to worry about what other people think of them or their actions. Many famous people have been bold in extreme circumstances. In fact, their boldness may have come out of a kind of desperation in hard times. Other people are bold in quiet ways, finding new ways to take on daily challenges of life without fear. Some people live every day of their life in a bold way. They are unafraid to be different from others or take chances.

What have you done in your life that you consider bold? What made you do it?

Boldness through Time

There have been many examples of boldness in the world. Here are a few:

- In a television series called *Star Trek*, the narrator spoke of "going boldly where no man has gone before." In this series, the crew of a spacecraft of the future traveled to new planets, meeting with new cultures and species. The crew was often in danger. Explorers through time have shown boldness in going to places nobody has ever visited. Explorers show both courage and a willingness to try something new. Famous people, like Sacagawea and Lewis and Clark, and everyday people who rode across America in wagon trains or moved to a new land across the sea have shown boldness.

- In the world of science, we move our knowledge forward by questioning existing ideas. Scientists have to think about new possibilities all the time. They risk failure, which requires them to be brave. Sometimes scientists are treated badly in their own lives. For example, Galileo went to prison for his theories about the solar system. But he made more life-changing discoveries in his lifetime than others made in hundreds of years.

Boldness requires taking risks. Can you think of examples in history or literature in which people took risks? Whether they succeeded or failed (as did Amelia Earhart in trying to fly around the world), we often think of them as heroes.

Being Bold in Life

Consider this situation:

> Noah was in charge of organizing a fund-raising drive for new band instruments. The students and teachers on the committee had agreed to hold a concert to raise money. However, everybody was worried whether people would attend and contribute.
>
> Noah got an idea. If he invited a popular jazz musician named Jose Ravel from a nearby city to perform, people would come. But somebody had to invite Ravel.
>
> Noah checked with the committee members, and they thought his idea was good. However, none of them was willing to ask because they thought the musician would never agree. Noah searched on the Internet and found Mr. Ravel's phone number. Nervously, he sat down that evening with a practiced speech in his head and started to dial.
>
> The next day he was happy to tell the committee that the jazz musician had been very nice to him and had agreed to perform at no charge. Everybody admired Noah's boldness.

Noah's idea was a bold way to promote the concert. Calling the popular musician required courage. Would you be able to pick up the phone and call somebody important to ask a question? Could you come up with creative ways to promote an event? Would you be bold in the same circumstances?

> **"** Whatever you can do or dream you can, begin it. Boldness has genius, power, and magic in it. **"**
> —Johann Wolfgang von Goethe, Poet and Dramatist

Being Bold in Practice

Find an example of somebody who has done something bold. Look in your local newspaper and news magazines or listen to the television news. Perhaps somebody has suggested a way to change how local government is run, even though others oppose her new ideas. Or maybe you can find an article about a local businessperson who has created new job opportunities for people by starting a new business against all odds.

What made this a bold act? What was the person risking? What did this person do that hadn't been tried before. Why did the act require courage?

BOLDNESS CHECKLIST

○ Be willing to try something nobody has tried before.

○ Be willing to fail and learn from your failure.

○ Don't worry too much about what people think of you.

○ Take on a challenge others have backed away from.

○ If your bold action involves others, consider the consequences to them before you act.

○ Don't be afraid to look a little foolish.

Bold Role Models

Here are some people who have a reputation for boldness or a bold act.

- Rosa Parks worked hard all her life as a field hand, seamstress, and domestic. On December 1, 1955, she was riding a bus home from work. When the bus filled up, she was expected to give her seat to a white man. Parks refused. She went to jail. By standing up against an unjust law, she showed courage. The black community boycotted the bus system for more than a year, at great hardship to themselves. Eventually, the boycott ended segregation on Montgomery, Alabama, busses.

- Isadora Duncan was a visionary dancer. She is credited with beginning modern dance. She boldly broke with the current approach to dance. Her theory of dance involved her attitudes toward social revolution and women's rights. Her willingness to invent, and not simply imitate, was the foundation of modern dance.

- At a time when it was illegal for women to attend university, Madame Marie Curie obtained an education by studying at night and earning money as a governess to study in another country. With an interest in science, she studied chemistry secretly at a local lab. Her hard work brought her to a university in Paris. She was the first woman in the world to earn a doctorate. She chose to investigate a field where little work had been done: radiation. Working with her husband, she discovered a new element called radium. Their work has been the basis for many advances in medical diagnosis. Curie was the first woman to win a Nobel Prize. Her courage and willingness to explore a new area showed a unique boldness.

What's in It for Me?

Consider these real-life consequences of being bold:

- Bold people may discover or invent something new and important to help, teach, or entertain people.

- Bold people try things very few people have tried before and are the first to experience the results.

- Bold people get opportunities others do not. The first person to go into space, climb Mt. Everest, or sail across the Atlantic Ocean could not have done so without boldness.

- A successful bold act may lead to a promotion at work. Even an unsuccessful bold act will show your employers you have the courage to take risks.

Related Words to Explore

Here are some words related to the trait of being bold and to its opposite:

- Strong
- Adventurous
- Brave
- Opinionated
- Definite

- Outspoken
- Decisive
- Timid
- Reserved
- Indecisive

CARING

Caring means feeling an interest in or affection for someone or something. Caring for other people can come easily when they are close to you. Caring for a parent or your friend is natural. But can you care for people you don't know? Do you care if somebody around the world is happy or sad? Caring people feel concern for others, whether or not they know them. They may also care about a cause, or animals, or the environment. It is sometimes hard for them to put boundaries on their caring because they naturally have an interest in others.

Are you a caring person?

What Does It Mean to Be Caring?

Caring is something most people do in small ways every day. A friend has a problem, so we listen and give advice. We take care of a pet by feeding it and showing it affection. We care about whether our friend does well in a school play. We are all caring people to some degree.

You will find caring people in all kinds of jobs and places. However, some people seem more caring than others. They don't care only for people they know. These people might become nurses or veterinarians or ministers. They like to help many people and may even do so for a living.

Caring through Time

There are many examples of organizations that have a mission of caring. Here are two of them:

- Societies such as the ASPCA (American Society for the Prevention of Cruelty to Animals) take care of animals. These groups work to fight cruelty to animals and to educate people about how to care for pets. Sometimes people do something that is bad for their pets without even knowing it. Did you know that leaving your dog in a parked car on a warm day could harm or kill it, for example? People who take pets into their homes should care enough about them to learn about their pets' care. Visit the ASPCA at www.aspca.org for more information.

- Habitat for Humanity volunteers build homes for those who can't afford to buy a house through traditional means. Community members come together and work with skilled people to build houses one by one. The group "seeks to eliminate poverty housing and homelessness from the world, and to make decent shelter a matter of conscience and action." The new homeowners participate in the building and put a down payment on the house. The people who volunteer materials and time for somebody they don't know care about people and their community. Visit www.Habitat.org for more about Habitat's mission.

What do you think people get from caring about others? Why do they give their time and attention? Do you want others to care about what happens to you? If you do, should you also care about them?

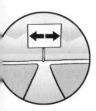

Being Caring in Life

Consider this situation:

> *Noelle had waited months to get tickets to a concert. The big day was coming, and she was getting very excited. The day would be twice as exciting because her mother was graduating from college with a master's degree. She had been going to school for five years. Noelle's mother was going to drop off her daughter at the concert on her way to the ceremony. Noelle would get a lift home for the family celebration that night.*
>
> *The afternoon of the big day, as Noelle and her mother were getting ready to leave, the phone rang. It was Susie, the babysitter, calling to say that her car broke down. She couldn't take care of Martin, Noelle's baby brother. In a panic, Noelle's mother called everybody she knew. Nobody was available to help. Looking very disappointed, her mother said she guessed she would have to miss the graduation ceremony. Noelle thought about offering to watch her baby brother, but it meant missing the concert.*

If you were Noelle, would you give up the concert to help your mother? It's likely that Noelle can go to another concert some day, but her mother will have only one graduation. What would you do?

> **"**Without a sense of caring there can be no sense of community.**"**
>
> —Anthony J. D'Angelo, Author

Being Caring in Practice

Look for examples of people being caring. Ask people you see being especially caring why they care about others. Does it make them feel good? Do they expect a reward or praise for doing it? Do they feel guilty if they don't care for others? Create a list of the answers. Then decide if one of these reasons matches your reason for caring.

Did you find that some people show an interest in others even when they would rather be doing something else? Nobody can be caring 24 hours a day. Sometimes we have to make ourselves take time to care. But whether or not it's an effort, our actions are what make us a caring person in our own and others' eyes.

CARING CHECKLIST

○ Show concern for people who are in pain.

○ Don't be mean or cruel to anybody.

○ Try to imagine what other people are feeling.

○ Be willing to sacrifice your own comfort to help others.

○ Provide comfort to people who need it.

○ Care for the earth and environment by recycling, not littering, and using natural resources wisely.

Caring Role Models

Here are some people from various walks of life. Each has a reputation for being caring.

- Princess Diana of England was involved in many charities and causes. She not only attended fundraising events, but went to poor and war-torn places. When she was among people, she showed concern and affection for them. Perhaps she helped others out of a sense of responsibility. Perhaps she was simply a caring person by nature. Her actions made her a caring person in the eyes of the world.

- Audrey Hepburn was a famous actress who became the Goodwill Ambassador for UNICEF. UNICEF is a part of the United Nations that supports children's causes. Hepburn was a victim of war as a child in Holland in World War II. She knew how hard poverty could be on children. She worked full time in the last five years of her life, traveling the world for UNICEF. She often was in difficult conditions to bring world attention to the cause of poor children.

- Paul Newman, another actor, started a corporation that makes food like popcorn and salad dressing. Newman donates all of the post-tax royalties he receives from the company to charities. He has given more than $150 million to educational and charitable groups. He founded The Hole in the Wall Gang Camp, where children with life-threatening illnesses can go.

If you had money and fame, would you take the time to care for others? If you were poor and worked hard all day, would you still take an interest in others? Caring people make the time for others because it adds value to their lives.

What's in It for Me?

Consider these real-life consequences of being a caring person:

- Caring people feel good about themselves.

- Caring people often find others care about them in return.

- Caring people help to make their communities better places to live.

- Caring people often make many friends in their lives.

Related Words to Explore

Here are some words related to the trait of caring and to its opposite:

- Concerned
- Kind
- Loving
- Nurturing

- Compassionate
- Uncaring
- Unfeeling
- Cold

> **"**You cannot do a kindness too soon because you never know how soon it will be too late.**"**
> —Ralph Waldo Emerson, Essayist and Poet

CAUTIOUS

Being cautious means that you are careful about taking risks and about trusting other people. You think about things before you do them. You don't put yourself in danger or do things that aren't safe.

Cautiousness is a tricky characteristic. Too much, and you are afraid to try anything new or trust anyone. Too little, and you could put yourself in dangerous situations again and again.

You should always try to balance caution with courage and trust. Are you cautious in the things you do?

What Does It Mean to Be Cautious?

Cautious people consider the consequences of their actions before they act. They weigh the pros and cons of various options. They are not easily fooled by dishonest people. They are careful in dangerous situations.

Being cautious means that you take time to think things through. You do not assume much.

Some caution can be helpful to everybody. But caution without courage can make you afraid to ever take action. Caution is a character trait that should be applied in moderation.

Cautiousness through Time

In military actions, countries have sometimes shown caution. But sometimes they have not shown enough caution before acting.

- Former U.S. Secretary of Defense Robert McNamara wrote, "U.S. intervention in Vietnam ignored warnings by intelligence experts and a thousand years of Vietnamese hostility to China…In the process we ignored the French experience and the strength of Vietnamese nationalism." McNamara said that by not considering all the facts and aspects of a culture, America entered a war that went on for years and ended in our withdrawal.

- In 1916, Woodrow Wilson ran for President in part on the campaign slogan "He kept us out of war." Wilson was a conservative who did not want America to jump into World War I. However, in April 1917, after careful consideration, then President Wilson asked Congress to declare war on Germany. He outlined 14 points for the war, including the establishment of the League of Nations after the war to ensure "territorial integrity" for all nations. Wilson not only took time to determine the right course of action, but he had thought forward to what would happen when the war was over. His caution probably delayed our entrance into World War I. Whether that was a good thing for our nation or world remains for historians to debate. But he did not let our nation act on impulse and in the heat of the moment.

Being Cautious in Life

Consider this situation:

Evan's friend Pete and his family asked him to go on a hiking and camping trip with them. Evan's father had taught him how to be cautious about potential dangers in the woods. He learned about the dangers of starting a fire in the forest and being careful about what to eat or drink.

The first day Pete's family hiked along the ridge of a gorge. It was a beautiful, sunny day. They had carried in a good supply of water, but as the warm day wore on, they drank a lot of it. That evening, they found a small pond and camped beside it. They cooked their dinner and were ready to settle down. Pete's father suggested that because they were low on water, he would fill up their water bottles with pond water. "It looks pretty clean," he said. Evan worried about that. The pond water might contain bacteria that could make them sick. His dad had told him to filter or boil the water before drinking it. He thought he should mention it but didn't want to embarrass Pete's dad.

Should Evan be cautious and talk to Pete's dad about the water? Should he just avoid drinking it himself and let the others take their chances? Sometimes being cautious means being cautious for others, too. What would be the price of not being cautious in this situation? Is it worth this risk to stay silent?

> **❝**Caution is the eldest child of wisdom.**❞**
> —**Victor Hugo, Poet and Novelist**

Being Cautious in Practice

Try thinking through all your significant actions for a whole day before you act. Make a list of pros and cons. Check the facts before you do anything. Don't commit to any promises until you have considered your options.

How did the day go? Did you avoid some problems by being more cautious than usual? Did you miss some opportunities by taking too much time to think things through? If you could write a sentence of advice to others about being cautious, what would it be?

CAUTIOUSNESS CHECKLIST

- ◯ Be careful about the situations you get yourself into.
- ◯ Think before you act.
- ◯ Don't trust people you don't know without checking the facts.
- ◯ Do trust people you know, but carefully consider what they are asking you to do.

Cautious Role Models

Here are some people who have a reputation for being cautious.

- Susan Butcher is a champion dog sledder who has won the famous Iditarod race three times. This 1,152-mile race across freezing Alaska wilderness is very challenging. "You have to be very selfless in your dedication to your dogs. When you come into a checkpoint, although there may be a wood stove to warm your feet by, you stay outside; you take care of your dogs, get them bedded down and fed. It may take three hours. Then you can go and have your 15 minutes inside," said Butcher. Although the race takes courage, it also takes caution to make sure the dogs and racer are taken care of.

- Harry Houdini was a master magician and escape artist. He was an athletic man who devised many dramatic escapes. He escaped from a straightjacket and from a locked box underwater. Houdini took great care to prepare for his escapes, always making sure the equipment in his act was working. A movie popularized the idea that he died during an escape. In fact, he died of a burst appendix, careful to the last not to make any mistakes in his act.

- Erik Weihenmeyer is one of the few people to have climbed Mt. Everest. The fact that he succeeded is even more remarkable considering he is blind. Erik had to be cautious about many things in preparing for and making his climb. "(I was) just putting one step in front of the next and trying to keep a very clear, focused mind, because I just knew that wasn't a place to make a mistake."

What's in It for Me?

Cautious people can reap many benefits. For example, they can

- Stay out of dangerous situations.
- Gather all the facts first and make educated decisions, which earns the respect of others.
- Avoid being taken advantage of.
- Feel confident in their choices.

Related Words to Explore

Here are some words related to the trait of being cautious and to its opposite:

- Careful
- Patient
- Concerned
- Moderate

- Unhurried
- Reckless
- Dangerous
- Impatient

> **"**The truth. It is a beautiful and terrible thing, and should therefore be treated with great caution.**"**
>
> —J.K. Rowling, **Author**

COMPASSIONATE

Compassionate people feel deeply for others. They feel sad when other people are in pain or unhappy. Compassionate people often choose careers in which they can take care of others, such as health care or social work.

When you see somebody who is suffering, what do you feel?

What Does It Mean to Be Compassionate?

If you see someone who is sick, sad, or upset, do you get upset, too? Do you think of ways you can help that person? If so, you may be compassionate. Compassionate people not only care about others, but usually do things to help them.

Perhaps compassionate people can put themselves in others' shoes and so feel their pain more easily than some. You may be more compassionate toward people who are going through a situation you've experienced. You identify with their feelings because you've had those same feelings.

Can you think of an example of a compassionate person in your family or school?

Compassion through Time

Compassion exists in history; for example:

- The Geneva Convention is a series of treaties among countries. These treaties, created in Geneva, Switzerland, establish international laws regarding the treatment of people during war. They are agreements among nations about the treatment of people wounded on the battlefield, treatment of prisoners of war, and treatment of civilians during wartime. The Geneva Convention is an attempt by several nations to show compassion and provide for humane treatment of people.

- Leprosy is a disease that causes disfigurement in those who suffer from it. Victims of the disease were originally kept apart from other people in fear that the disease was contagious. Several people worked hard to get lepers medical care and to find cures, even though they sometimes got the disease themselves.

Compassion involves putting yourself in somebody else's place. It involves understanding how that person must feel. More than that, compassion causes you to act to help others.

> **"** *Until he extends the circle of his compassion to all living things, man will not himself find peace.* **"**
> —Albert Schweitzer, Mission Doctor and Theologian

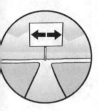

Being Compassionate in Life

Consider this situation:

One day when Cammie was walking home from school, she spotted a small dog lying on the side of the road. It didn't move as she walked by, but sat there shivering. She noticed that the dog was very thin, and its fur was dirty.

Cammie approached the dog cautiously, holding out her hand and bending over to show that she wasn't a threat. The dog stood up shakily and came to her, licking her hand. It had no tags and looked hungry. Cammie was afraid that the dog might get sick outdoors in the snowstorm that was predicted. So, she untied the ribbon that held her books together and made a kind of leash to lead the dog home. When she arrived, she told her mother about how she had found the dog. Together, they called the animal shelter.

The man at the shelter said a week earlier a family had lost a dog that matched this dog's description. Cammie and her mother took the dog to the shelter, where his family claimed him.

Being compassionate toward people or animals doesn't always bring us a reward, beyond feeling good that we could be of help. Some people might have passed by the dog. What would you have done? Why?

Being Compassionate in Practice

Today try to focus on one person who seems unhappy. Find ways to understand that person's pain and to sympathize with him. Show compassion to the person by helping or reassuring him.

Even if this person is not a close friend, can you find ways to care about him just because he is in pain?

COMPASSION CHECKLIST

○ Try to feel what others must be feeling.

○ Imagine what it would feel like if you were in another person's position.

○ Don't look for reward. Just help people in trouble or pain.

○ Help those you sense need help.

○ Appreciate the differences among all people.

Compassionate Role Models

Here are people with a reputation for being compassionate.

- Louise Arbour is a Canadian who was the chief prosecutor of war crimes in Rwanda and the former Yugoslavia. She worked as part of an international tribunal to bring criminals to trial. Arbour has been described as standing up for victims with courage and compassion. As the U.N. High Commissioner of Human Rights, she works for compassionate treatment of all people.

- Jong-Wook Lee is a Korean physician who has worked for years to help solve population-sized health problems that claim tens of thousands of lives. He studies areas where disease hurts many people. This field is called public health. He made a commitment to get as much treatment as possible for the 40 million people infected with AIDS worldwide.

Compassion results in many types of actions. Sometimes compassionate people view injustice and stand up for the victims of that injustice. Sometimes compassionate people work to relieve suffering and pain. Who or what are you willing to fight for because you feel compassion for their suffering?

> **"**If you want others to be happy, practice compassion. If you want to be happy, practice compassion.**"**
> —The Dalai Lama, Spiritual Leader

What's in It for Me?

Consider these real-life consequences of being compassionate:

- People admire you for showing concern for others.

- You may find a job as a doctor, social worker, or human rights activist.

- Your compassion keeps you from hurting other people.

- If you can act on your compassion, you change the world for the better.

Related Words to Explore

Here are some words related to the trait of being compassionate and to its opposite:

- Sympathetic
- Empathetic
- Feeling
- Caring
- Concerned

- Kindhearted
- Unfeeling
- Cruel
- Impervious

> **"**The most important thing in any relationship is not what you get but what you give.**"**
> —Eleanor Roosevelt, First Lady and Activist

CONSIDERATE

To be considerate means to think of others—their feelings and their welfare. Considerate people not only think about others' feelings, but they also act in the interest of others.

Are there people who are considerate of your feelings? How do they make you feel?

What Does It Mean to Be Considerate?

When you make a decision, do you take into account other people who are involved? Do you take action based on how you will affect others? Or do you think only about your feelings?

Considerate people take the time to think about how their words or actions or attitudes will make others feel. They may choose a career based on how their work may affect others.

As you go through your day, how often do you think about what other people think and feel? Are you a considerate person?

Consideration through Time

There have been many examples of consideration in the world, including these:

- Diplomats are in the business of considering others' feelings and customs. They represent their country to another country. In this role, they have to understand the other country's customs and attitudes and act in a way that will not give offense. Diplomacy was practiced as long ago as the fourteenth century B.C. in Egypt. Diplomats often negotiate treaties and other agreements between nations.

- Some nations or groups of people refuse to do business with countries that employ child labor. People who do not want to contribute to the mistreatment of children will boycott (refuse to deal with) these countries. They show their consideration for children through these actions.

Consideration simply means thinking about the other person. Whether that means you act in a very polite and kind manner or you take a stand to protect other people, it is the act of thinking about others that is important. Who are you considerate of?

> **"** Remember there's no such thing as a small act of kindness. Every act creates a ripple with no logical end. **"**
> —Scott Adams, Cartoonist

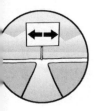

Being Considerate in Life

Consider this situation:

Mario got home from school and went immediately to the kitchen for a snack. He turned on the stereo to listen to his new CD. Mario's mother, who had stayed home from work that day because she wasn't feeling well, came downstairs after a few minutes. She asked him about his day and made sure he knew there were fresh apples in the refrigerator.

After a few minutes, Mario's mom said she was still not feeling well, so she headed back upstairs to sleep. As she went upstairs, Mario realized the music might prevent his mom from sleeping. He turned off the music and started chopping some vegetables to make a pizza for dinner so his mom wouldn't have to cook.

Consideration can show itself in small ways. If you think about how others are feeling and do things to make them feel better, you are considerate.

> **"**Being considerate of others will take your children further in life than any college degree.**"**
> —Marian Wright Edelman, Founder and President of the Children's Defense Fund

Being Considerate in Practice

Think of one person in your life whose feelings you should consider. Pick an opportunity to act considerate toward that person. Think about his or her feelings and act accordingly.

How did that person react to your consideration?

CONSIDERATION CHECKLIST

◯ Think about how others feel before you act.

◯ Don't do anything to others you wouldn't want them to do to you.

◯ Do things that will make other people feel better.

◯ Think about the consequences of your actions.

> **"**Really big people are, above everything else, courteous, considerate, and generous—not just to some people in some circumstances—but to everyone all the time.**"**
> —Thomas J. Watson, Business Executive

Considerate Role Models

Here are people with a reputation for being considerate.

- Emily Post was born in Baltimore, Maryland, in 1872. She wrote newspaper articles and stories for magazines. Her publisher asked her to write a book about *etiquette*, another word for *manners*. For many years, the book was a huge success, outlining rules for the way people should behave with each other. Post believed that proper behavior was an outcome of common sense and consideration of people. The book is still published today, with updates for modern thought by her relative, Elizabeth Post.

- Dag Hammarskjold was a Swedish-born diplomat who had a lot to do with the growth of the influence of the United Nations. People talk about him as quiet and tactful, and as somebody who was able to consider all sides in peace negotiations. His policies encouraged people to cooperate with each other. His work with people of many nations required that he consider many sides of an issue.

People who are considerate usually respect others and believe they are entitled to good treatment. Whether consideration results in simple human courtesy or in helping an entire society to achieve its goals, it is an important part of the way we treat others.

> **"**Constant kindness can accomplish much. As the sun makes ice melt, kindness causes misunderstanding, mistrust, and hostility to evaporate.**"**
> —**Albert Schweitzer, Physician and Humanitarian**

What's in It for Me?

Consider these real-life consequences of being considerate:

- Considerate people think about others' feelings. As a result, they do things to make others feel better.

- Considerate people impress others with their kindness.

- Considerate people cause others to be more considerate of them.

- Being considerate helps you avoid conflict because you have anticipated others' feelings and concerns.

Related Words to Explore

Here are some words related to the trait of being considerate and to its opposite:

- Thoughtful
- Kind
- Understanding
- Caring
- Selfless

- Polite
- Thoughtless
- Inconsiderate
- Rude

COOPERATIVE

Cooperative people throughout history have made a significant difference in the world. They understand that the power of many people working together can be great. Cooperative people focus on a common goal rather than individual differences.

Are you cooperative with your friends or family?

What Does It Mean to Be Cooperative?

When people cooperate, they can achieve great things. Separately, they may have little power or resources, but together they can accomplish much more.

Cooperative people understand this. They are able to work with others to reach a common goal. Cooperation requires that you put your ego and needs aside and find ways to work with others. Lack of cooperation often causes problems and arguments.

Would you rather be cooperative and get along with people or be uncooperative and fight with others?

   Young Person's Character Education Handbook, © JIST Life

Cooperation through Time

Here are examples of cooperation in history:

- The crew of Apollo 13 had some serious challenges. An explosion in space resulted in loss of oxygen, water, electrical power, and the propulsion system the crew needed to get back to Earth. Working with hundreds of engineers and scientists back on Earth, the crew had to scramble to survive. Keeping calm under incredible pressure, the astronauts moved to an escape module. Both the people on the ground at NASA and the astronauts in space cooperated to conquer a set of problems never encountered before.

- The countries of Europe decided in 1993 to establish a European Union. This union of 25 independent countries was founded on political, economic, and social cooperation. The countries involved are committed to working together for peace and prosperity, rather than remaining entirely separate.

Cooperation can occur among a handful of people or among nations. It happens when people realize that working together can get them more than working separately. Cooperative people see more benefit in working with others. In addition, they may be more able to make compromises than others.

> **"**Leadership is based on inspiration, not domination; on cooperation, not intimidation.**"**
> —William Arthur Wood, Secretary of a Charity Organization for the Poor

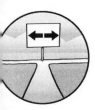

Being Cooperative in Life

Consider this situation:

> *Mr. Spitzer was the seventh-grade science teacher. He divided his class into two groups to do a science project.*
>
> *The first group was made up of kids who could never agree on anything. After a few weeks of working on the project, these students had little to show for their efforts.*
>
> *The second group included Naomi. She had learned a lot about cooperation from her grandfather, who was a basketball coach. Naomi encouraged the other kids to cooperate and work together to complete the project. After a couple of weeks, these students presented Mr. Spitzer with a working model of their project.*

Cooperation gets things done. Lack of cooperation uses energy in fighting and disagreeing. Are you a cooperative person?

> **"**Power consists in one's capacity to link his will with the purpose of others, to lead by reason and a gift of cooperation.**"**
>
> **—Woodrow Wilson, President**

Being Cooperative in Practice

Pick a project that involves other people either in your family or at school. Don't think about yourself. Instead, think about how you can do what will help everybody reach the goal. If somebody asks you to help, do so. Focus on getting the job done and getting along with others.

COOPERATION CHECKLIST

- ⬭ Work with others to reach a common goal.
- ⬭ Don't focus on your own needs. Instead, focus on the needs of the group.
- ⬭ Look for ways to resolve differences between you and others.
- ⬭ Don't fight with others. Find things you have in common.
- ⬭ Encourage people to work together to achieve great things.

Cooperative Role Models

Here are people in with a reputation for being cooperative.

- When Linus Torvalds was a college student, he started an Internet discussion group to build a free computer operating system. He wanted to build a system with the cooperation of many individuals. His goal was to make the code for the system freely available to all. The resulting system, Linux, grew through the efforts of thousands of people who took the underlying code and added their own contributions to it.

- Millard Fuller and his wife, Linda, founded Habitat for Humanity International. The group brings together community members to build housing for the poor. Homeowner families are expected to work alongside volunteers to build their homes. This model of cooperation for building affordable housing for the poor has spread around the world.

When people cooperate, they can accomplish great things. They can build technology or new homes, businesses or spaceships. Have you ever worked with others to build something worthwhile? How did that feel?

What's in It for Me?

Consider these real-life consequences of being cooperative:

- People admire you for working well with others.

- On the job, others see you as someone who can work as part of a team.

- You can be part of great accomplishments that involve many people's efforts.

- You don't waste time fighting others but find ways to work together.

Related Words to Explore

Here are some words related to the trait of being cooperative and to its opposite:

- Helpful
- Supportive
- Obliging
- Accommodating
- Team player

- Trusting
- Uncooperative
- Contentious
- Loner

COURAGEOUS

Being courageous means being able to overcome fear. Courage is something we all have in some measure. How courageous we are and under what circumstances varies. You may be very brave about some things but have difficulty overcoming your fears about others. Are you courageous about traveling to new, strange places but afraid of spiders? Do you find it easy to try a new sport but difficult to talk to new people? It's important to understand what frightens you and learn to control your fears.

Are you a courageous person?

What Does It Mean to Be Courageous?

Don't make the mistake of thinking that courageous people aren't afraid of anything. They have fears, just like everybody. However, they can overcome their fears and keep going in spite of them. People who lack courage in a specific situation may panic or run away. People with courage may feel like running. Instead, they take control of their fears and continue to face the situation and take action.

Courage isn't only about big, heroic acts. Of course, people who fight fires or rescue people have courage. But it also takes courage to go to your first day in a new school, or to stand up in front of a group and give a speech, or to try a new sport.

Look for courage in all sorts of people and all sorts of situations, and you'll find it all around you.

Courageousness through Time

Here are some examples of situations that require courage:

- Firefighters put themselves in danger every day. They go into buildings that were built under a wide variety of fire codes. When they do, they never know whether the structures will hold up or fall apart. Every fire is different, so they face unknown dangers in every location. Although firefighters always prepare by having the right equipment and protective clothing, they are often in deadly situations. In large emergencies, such as the 9-11 attacks on the World Trade Center in New York City, they have to deal with many people who are hurt or panicking. They have to help others while containing the danger from fire. Their calm example saves lives.

- People who attempt a sport such as skydiving or mountain climbing are in danger. They get the satisfaction of mastering a new skill, and perhaps they find the risk to be thrilling. Still, they have fears to overcome. Often, they have to support others on their team and help them come safely home. People who help those in danger take on not only the physical danger to themselves, but the responsibility for others. One example is rangers who rescue skiers in trouble.

Someone can show courage by putting himself in a dangerous situation to help others, or even by tackling something new for fun, such as sky diving. Is one form of courage better than another? If you combine courage with compassion or cautiousness, two other traits discussed in this book, how might courage change?

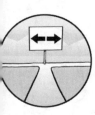

Being Courageous in Life

Consider this situation:

> *Calli's friend Sara asked her to go into the city with her on Saturday to shop. They caught the 9:15 train and arrived downtown on time. They shopped all morning and decided to stop at a burger place for lunch. The lunch came and they ate. When they were done, Sara went up to the cashier to pay. As they walked out of the restaurant, Sara checked her change. She realized that the cashier had made change for $15, not the $20 that she had given her. Without that money, Sara and Calli couldn't afford to get the train tickets home.*
>
> *The girls went back inside and told the cashier about the mistake. She glared at them and told them she never made mistakes like that. The girls walked over to the corner near the entrance, not knowing what to do. "Should we call my folks?" said Sara. Calli knew Sara's folks would be unhappy at having to drive in and out of the city at this time of day. "What else can we do?" she asked. "We can go back and ask to speak to the manager," said Calli. Sara was terrified at the suggestion. "That lady will call the police or something!" she moaned. "No," said Calli reassuringly, even though she was scared to confront the cashier herself, "it will be okay." The girls turned and went back to the cashier.*

Calli was nervous about confronting an adult regarding this misunderstanding, but she considered the alternatives. Making either of their parents drive an hour each way to pick them up would be difficult. She knew they were in the right. She considered the worst that could happen was that the cashier could yell at them. Was Calli courageous? How would you act in a similar situation?

Being Courageous in Practice

Think of something you have been wanting to do but were afraid to try. Perhaps you want to make friends with somebody but aren't sure that person will like you. Or maybe you want to learn a new sport but aren't sure you'll be good at it. Write down a list of all the bad things that could happen if you tried to do this thing and failed. Now write a list of what could happen if you tried and succeeded.

What is the worst thing that could happen to you? What would you get from taking on the challenge, even if you failed? How would you feel if you never acted? How would you feel if you tackled the challenge and succeeded?

Deciding to show courage sometimes happens when we realize that the worst that could happen to us isn't all that bad.

COURAGEOUSNESS CHECKLIST

- ○ Consider the consequences of actions, but don't let that stop you from acting.

- ○ Don't run away from situations or things that frighten you.

- ○ Consider fears you have conquered in the past and gain courage from your successes.

- ○ Learn to control your fear, and not the other way around.

- ○ Use your courage to help others.

Courageous Role Models

Here are some people who have a reputation for being courageous.

- Berthe Fraser was a housewife living in France at the beginning of World War II. Eventually, she became the woman at the center of an underground network that saved many British lives. She engineered the escape of hundreds of British soldiers in the early years of the war until she was caught. She was sent to prison camp for 15 months. As soon as she was released, she began her activities again. She provided shelter, transportation, and safe places from which agents could perform their missions. In 1944, the Germans captured and tortured her every day for 23 weeks. She never gave the names of her contacts in the Resistance movement. On September 1, 1944, American and English soldiers stormed her prison and freed her from her chains. She showed remarkable courage in a dangerous time.

- Polar explorer Ann Bancroft fought bitter circumstances to lead the first all-female expedition to the South Pole. However, when asked about the courage this took, she told one interviewer that it took much more courage for her to deal with her dyslexia. This is a condition that makes it difficult to read. When she was in college, she was told that she should give up trying to get a teaching certification and simply get her degree. Because Ann wanted to teach, she took a stand with her student advisor. She said she would do what it took to get her teaching credentials. Later, during her expedition to the South Pole, she would compare her difficulties with the challenges of completing school and realize the expedition was easy in comparison.

What's in It for Me?

Courageous people can reap many benefits. For example, they can

- Become more comfortable with the challenges life presents and experience less stress.

- Help others by their example.

- Become respected and trusted to stand up to difficult situations.

- Receive rewards of money or fame because of their courageous acts.

Related Words to Explore

Here are some words related to the trait of being courageous and to its opposite:

- Brave
- Adventurous
- Bold
- Gutsy

- Strong
- Timid
- Afraid
- Scared

> **"** *Life shrinks or expands in proportion to one's courage.* **"**
> —Anais Nin, Author

CREATIVE

Creativity exists in us all. But truly creative people make a habit of coming up with new and interesting things. Often we think of artists when we hear the word *creative*. But a businessperson coming up with a new way to market a product is creative. A teacher who thinks of a new way to help children learn is creative. A cook putting together ingredients to create a new recipe is creative.

In what ways are you creative?

What Does It Mean to Be Creative?

Creativity is defined as bringing something new into being. That something new could be almost anything: an idea, a painting, a piece of music, or an invention. The important thing is that it is new and original to the creator.

That's not to say that creative people don't borrow and build on others' ideas and work. They do. Musicians often compose music that is in part based on another piece of music, but they change it in some way. Writers get ideas from other writers, but they put their own spin on those ideas.

To be creative, you have to be willing to try something completely new. Trying something new means you have to be willing to take the risk that what you create might not succeed. Creative people find excitement and pleasure in exploring new things. That pleasure outweighs the risk of failure.

Creativity through Time

Creativity is apparent in many types of art, for example:

- Science fiction is a type of writing in which the writer imagines worlds that don't exist. Often science fiction involves alien life forms and other worlds. Sometimes devices such as time travel or special powers are used to make the impossible possible. The best examples of science fiction writing are very creative and challenge readers to think beyond what they know. Sometimes science fiction imaginings turn into reality. It's possible that early writings about life on other planets inspired our landing on the moon and sending probes to Mars.

- *Theater of the Absurd* is a term given to the work of a collection of playwrights including Samuel Beckett and Eugene Ionesco. In these plays, metaphor is used to express the playwrights' feelings. (Metaphor is one thing that is used to represent another.) For example, in Ionesco's play *Rhinoceros*, he represents concerns about government control over the individual. He does this by showing the people of a town turning into rhinoceroses. The creative images can sometimes be more powerful than a more realistic type of theater. Theater of the Absurd requires the people watching the plays to make a creative leap of imagination, as well.

The best creative works of art make the person experiencing them think and question things they took for granted. Do you think any work of art is creative? Are works of art that are very different from anything else that's come before more creative than those that are similar to others? Is the act of creating something new in itself creative, or must the outcome of the act be unique?

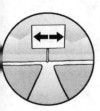

Being Creative in Life

Consider this situation:

> *Juanita Gooding, the drama teacher, was busy directing the school musical when the principal asked her to have the third period drama students put on a short skit at the assembly in March. Ms. Gooding knew she couldn't spend much time helping them, so she asked the students to work on the skit independently. She suggested they might take the fairy tale of Jack and the Beanstalk and write a short play based on it.*

> *The kids got together one afternoon to kick around ideas. Most of the kids just wanted to create a play that followed the original story. Carrie had a different idea. "What if instead of just doing the story like it is, we put the giant on trial? His lawyer could argue that Jack trespassed and stole things from him. Jack's lawyer could argue that the giant had hurt lots of people and deserved to have his stuff stolen."*

> *Mickey was worried. "That's not what Ms. Gooding told us to do. We'll get in trouble." The students talked it over, but in the end Carrie convinced them to try the different approach. They had a lot of fun coming up with the skit. However, they were a little worried Ms. Gooding would be angry or that nobody would like the play. As they marched on stage at the assembly, they were all excited but a little nervous.*

What risks would you take to do something creative? Do you think the teacher liked what the students did? What was creative about the idea? Would you be brave enough to think of a new way of doing something and then try it?

Being Creative in Practice

Think of something you feel strongly about. Perhaps you might think of a person you care about or something in your life that frightens you or makes you sad. Now create something that represents that feeling. You can paint something, write some music, build a machine, or write a story. Make anything you like, as long as it's new.

How did you choose what you would make? How does it represent your feelings? If you showed it to somebody who doesn't know you, do you think he or she would know what feeling inspired it? Ask three people what they think your work represents. You might be surprised to hear that they see or hear different things. The reason is that people bring their own experiences and ideas to creative works. There-fore, they come to different conclusions. Because we all see things differently, we are all creative in our own way.

CREATIVITY CHECKLIST

- ⬭ Dare to try something completely new.
- ⬭ Turn your ideas about something upside down or inside out.
- ⬭ Imagine what it would be like if something were the opposite of what you assume it to be.
- ⬭ Don't worry too much about whether people will approve of what you create.
- ⬭ Create things that express your feelings or ideas.
- ⬭ Challenge other people to think differently about something.

Creative Role Models

Here are some people from various walks of life. Each has a reputation for creativity.

- Lewis Carroll wrote *Alice in Wonderland*. In that book, Alice falls down a hole, entering another world. That world is filled with creatures like a talking cat that disappears and reappears and a six-foot-tall rabbit. Carroll was actually a professor of mathematics. His books include his opinions about Victorian society expressed in symbols and metaphors.

- Walt Disney was a very creative man whose approach to entertainment continues to charm new generations. Mickey Mouse was one of his earliest creations. Later, he ran a motion picture studio whose artists created feature-length animations, such as *Snow White and the Seven Dwarves*. He had the idea to create an amusement park called Disneyland. Though some of his creations were based on fairy tales written by others, the combination of animation, music, and those stories was unique and beautiful.

- Andre Norton wrote science fiction and fantasy books, short stories, and poetry. She took the first name Andre because few women writers created science fiction at the time, and the male-sounding name made her work more acceptable. She wrote 35 books in one popular series called *Witch World*. She imagined many new worlds and colorful creatures, and she often placed a young hero in her stories.

What's in It for Me?

Consider these real-life consequences of being creative:

- You can experience things nobody else experiences because only you could have created them.

- You may be a good problem solver if you don't get defeated by what is, but imagine what could be.

- If you create things, you leave a legacy to the world that is unique.

- You may receive awards or fame for your creations.

- At work, creative people help make productive changes in the way things are done every day.

Related Words to Explore

Here are some words related to the trait of being creative and to its opposite:

- Imaginative
- Original
- Artistic
- Inspired
- Visionary

- Inventive
- Uncreative
- Unimaginative
- Uninspired
- Dull

DECISIVE

Being decisive in part means being able to make decisions. Decisive people can not only make decisions, but they can also make them quickly and under extreme pressure. Then they enforce those decisions without frequently changing their minds.

Decisive people tend to become leaders. Others respect their ability to make a choice and stick by it. Sometimes they are right, and sometimes they are wrong. However, they never fail through hesitating to make some kind of choice.

Have you been decisive in your life?

What Does It Mean to Be Decisive?

A decisive person recognizes that making a choice in a positive manner often leads to success. Every choice risks failure, but every choice also offers the possibility of success. Hesitating to make a choice can lead to problems or even disaster. After you commit to a choice, you can take action and sometimes change course to reach your goal. Never committing to a choice almost always results in failure.

Being decisive carries with it great responsibility. By being the person to make a choice, you are also the person who others follow. If your choice is not right, others may suffer. Therefore, although decisive people can make quick decisions, they should not make them without considering the risks to themselves and others.

Decisiveness through Time

Here are some examples of decisiveness:

- The automobile industry has gone through good and bad times. Challenges come from changes in technology, government regulations, and competition. Lee Iacocca has been president of both Ford and Chrysler. During his time at Ford, Iacocca introduced the Mustang model and the minivan. Introducing a new car to the market is risky. It can pay off in big ways, though. At Chrysler, Iacocca saved the failing company by making tough decisions. He turned the company around and paid off all its debts. He even cut his own salary to $1 a year to provide an example to other managers. In business, studying a problem and then making decisions are important to success.

- Bill Gates was just starting his company when he was approached with a new idea in 1979. A programmer named Tim Patterson had created an operating system called 86-DOS. He went to IBM with the idea for use in the company's computers, but IBM wasn't interested. When Gates saw the program, he made the decision to buy it for $100,000. At the time, this was a great deal of money for Gates, but the purchase paid off. MS-DOS was the most popular operating system for many years; IBM used it in all its computers starting in 1981. DOS grew into the Windows operating system. This and other programs used with Windows have made Gates into a billionaire.

Being Decisive in Life

Consider this situation:

Colin and Marcus had been best friends for years. In their junior year of high school, their parents encouraged them to think about college plans. Colin knew he had to get a good SAT score to be accepted into a good school, so he worked with a tutor. He looked over information on schools and chose three that he liked. Then he began to fill out applications. When the cost of one school turned out to be too high for his parents, he got online and found a scholarship that could help him pay tuition.

Meanwhile, Marcus couldn't decide whether he wanted to go to college or take a year off. He looked at the school brochures his mother got for him, but he didn't know if he wanted to major in history or computers. Therefore, he didn't know which school would be best. Because he couldn't decide on a school, he missed the early submission deadline. When he finally turned in a couple of applications just before the final deadline, he had lost out of scholarship money and wasn't accepted by either school. He had no choice but to go to the junior college in town, which had no history program and a weak computer program.

Not making decisions can snowball. You put off one decision, and you miss out on opportunities. By the time you make a decision, it's too late. Have you been in situations in which you wish you had made a decision more quickly? If you put off making certain decisions about your own future, could you miss out on some opportunities altogether?

Being Decisive in Practice

Think of an issue you have been trying to resolve. Make a decision about what to do. Then do it. Don't change your mind or give up, but follow through based on your decision. How did it feel? Was making the decision a relief? Were you tempted to change your mind partway through? What rewards or problems did you encounter by sticking by your decision?

DECISIVENESS CHECKLIST

- ◯ Make choices with conviction.
- ◯ Weigh options, but make decisions without delay.
- ◯ Go with your gut instincts instead of getting hung up with analyzing multiple choices.
- ◯ Realize that no option is foolproof, and that usually action is better than inaction.
- ◯ Accept the consequences of your choices.

❝To know just what has to be done, then do it, comprises the whole philosophy of practical life.❞
—Sir William Osler, Physician

Decisive Role Models

Here are people from various walks of life. Each has a reputation for decisiveness.

- Margaret Thatcher was known as the "iron lady" because she stood strongly by her decisions. The daughter of a grocer and dressmaker, she became the first female prime minister of England. She won three terms as prime minister, the longest-serving prime minister since 1827. Thatcher faced many decisions, including the choice to help the former British territory of Zimbabwe (Rhodesia) become independent from England in 1980 and going to war over British rule of the Falkland Islands south of Argentina in 1982. Ms. Thatcher always seemed to be clear thinking and definite in her choices, a hallmark of a decisive person.

- Julius Caesar ruled the Roman Empire from 100 B.C. to 44 B.C. In part, the real history of his dictatorship over Rome is unknown. It is clear, however, that he took charge during a turbulent time in history. He worked through legal systems to make change. He expanded the participation of colonies in government. He improved the world from Africa to Corinth with bridges, aqueducts, and roads. He created public libraries and stabilized the economy. He also did many things that were less admirable, but he was always strong in his choices, even defying current wisdom in his actions.

Decisive people are often leaders. If they make bad decisions, they will not be well remembered. If they make good decisions, they are much admired. What do you think this statement means: Sometimes it seems that the ability to make a decision and follow through with it is more important than which decision you make.

What's in It for Me?

Decisive people can reap many benefits. For example, they can

- Lead people into new ventures.

- Be recognized as strong people with leadership qualities.

- Become managers in work situations.

- Feel confident in their choices.

- Experience less stress about making decisions than more indecisive people.

Related Words to Explore

Here are some words related to the trait of being decisive and to its opposite:

- Resolute
- Clear thinking
- Positive
- Certain

- Determined
- Uncertain
- Indecisive
- Vacillating

> **"**If I had to sum up in one word what makes a good manager, I'd say decisiveness. You can have the fanciest computers to gather the numbers, but in the end you have to set a timetable and act.**"**
>
> —Lee Iacocca, Businessman

DEDICATED

Dedicated people commit to something that's important to them. Commitment means that they are loyal and will spend a lot of time and effort on the thing they are dedicated to. Some people might be dedicated to a cause, to helping people, or to their work. Other people are dedicated to a hobby such as performing in their local community theater or running the local farmers' market.

Is there something in your life you are dedicated to?

What Does It Mean to Be Dedicated?

Dedication involves focusing on something that's very important to you. An artist might be dedicated to her art, an animal lover might be dedicated to animal rights, a parent is dedicated to his children. Dedication usually involves regularly thinking about and working for a cause or person.

Dedicated people often are passionate about the thing they are dedicated to. Because strong emotions can be involved, some people get so dedicated to causes they do bad things in the name of it. If you dedicate yourself to something, you should balance that dedication with common sense and other activities and relationships in your life.

Have you ever known somebody who was dedicated? Could you imagine that person giving up the thing he or she was dedicated to? Have you ever been dedicated to anything?

Young Person's Character Education Handbook, © JIST Life

Dedication through Time

Throughout history, people have been dedicated to causes, for example:

- During World War II, people in the French Resistance were committed to do what they could to defeat the Germans. Because they were under German rule, they had to act in secret. They worked to provide help to Allied soldiers behind enemy lines. They also provided information about enemy plans to the British and Americans. Even though they were in danger every minute, they kept going because of their dedication to defeating the Germans.

- In World War II, Japanese pilots named kamikazes were so dedicated to their cause that they were willing to fly their planes into enemy ships at sea. In the process, they damaged the ships and died. This extreme dedication may have been a result of both their love of country and their military training.

Choosing what things you will dedicate yourself to says interesting things about you. What do you feel you should spend your life doing? What will you get out of the time and energy you put in? Are you dedicated to something that helps others or that makes you feel good? Can you ever be too dedicated, or dedicated to the wrong thing? Is it right that some people are so dedicated they are willing to die for that cause?

Being Dedicated in Life

Consider this situation:

> *Scott had loved animals ever since he was a little kid. His family had two dogs, a cat, and a hamster. He belonged to 4-H and participated in his club's activities at the county fair.*
>
> *After the local animal shelter gave a presentation at his school and said it needed volunteers, Scott asked his mother if he could help. She said he could volunteer at the shelter for a couple of hours each week. However, she didn't want him to neglect his schoolwork. Scott started working at the shelter walking and feeding the dogs. He enjoyed the work so much that he started spending four or five hours a week there. His schoolwork began to suffer.*
>
> *One evening, Scott's parents sat him down to talk about his grades. He admitted he had been putting more time than he should have at the shelter, on top of his 4-H work. His parents told him they were proud of his helping animals, but he was spending too much time on them. Then his dad pointed out that if Scott wanted to make a living working with animals, he'd have to get good grades at school. Scott agreed to cut back on his volunteer hours, and his parents agreed to help him look into what it takes to have a career working with animals.*

Part of being dedicated is occasionally getting carried away with something. Dedication can make you do tremendous things, but it should not take over your life. Do you spend more time on something than anything else? Has that ever caused problems in other parts of your life?

Being Dedicated in Practice

What do you care most about in your life? What would you be willing to spend a lifetime doing? Try to pick one thing you think is very important. Then identify ways you might dedicate yourself to it. Does it make you happy to think of spending time on this thing? What rewards and challenges would dedicating yourself bring?

DEDICATION CHECKLIST

○ Determine what is important to you, and devote a large measure of your energy to it.

○ Even when it is difficult to continue with something you value, stay committed to it.

○ Don't give up when things go wrong.

○ Stay loyal to the thing or person you are dedicated to.

○ Be willing to make your commitment clear to others.

"The person who makes a success of living is the one who sees his goal steadily and aims for it unswervingly. That is dedication.**"**

—Cecil B. DeMille, Film Director

Dedicated Role Models

Here are some people from various walks of life. Each has a reputation for being dedicated:

- Martin Luther King, Jr., was an important figure in the Civil Rights Movement in the 1950s and 1960s in America. He was a minister who worked for peaceful protest against discrimination. He helped to lead boycotts and marches to raise awareness of the condition of black people, especially in the South. Even when he and others were the victims of police beatings and arrests, he kept working on his cause. He won the Nobel Peace Prize for his non-violent efforts.

- Mother Teresa is an example of religious dedication. At age 17, she became a Catholic missionary nun. She worked her entire life helping the poor and sick around the world. She established homes for people with AIDS and other diseases. When she won the Nobel Peace Prize for her efforts, she asked that the $6,000 that was to be spent on a banquet in her honor be donated to the poor.

- Mahatma Gandhi worked through nonviolent means to end British rule in India. He was devoted to the well-being of his people and the end of racism in India. He believed that spiritual things should be expressed through everyday activities and the way people live their lives. He lived very simply, even though he became famous throughout the world. His devotion to peaceful change has been an inspiration to many, including Martin Luther King, Jr.

What's in It for Me?

Consider these real-life consequences of being dedicated:

- You may support a cause that helps others or improves the world.

- You may gain skills you can apply in other areas of your life.

- You will meet people with similar interests.

- You will feel the pleasure of accomplishment.

- You have a focus in your life that keeps you going in tough times.

Related Words to Explore

Here are some words related to the trait of being dedicated and to its opposite:

- Devoted
- Enthusiastic
- Committed
- Loyal
- Faithful

- Staunch
- Unfaithful
- Uncommitted
- Fanatical

> **"**The long-term study of people who eventually became wealthy clearly reveals that their 'luck' arose from dedication they had to an arena they enjoyed.**"**
> —Srully Blotnick, Psychologist

DEPENDABLE

Being dependable means that if you make a promise, you do everything you can to keep it. You hate to disappoint other people. Dependable people may not be flashy. They often move behind the scenes to make sure things happen as planned. But they are often the people who make the difference between success and failure.

Have you ever depended on people to do what they said they would?

What Does It Mean to Be Dependable?

If a friend says she will help you and doesn't come through, you will hesitate to depend on her again. If the person who is working on a project with you shows up late time after time, you will tend not to depend on him in the future. People who don't do what they say they will are undependable.

On the other hand, people who always do what they say they will are dependable. You can trust them. Even when they cannot do what they promised because something unexpected happens, they always let you know the problem so you can do something to make things right. Undependable people don't communicate when there is a problem and don't show up when they said they would.

Everyone is dependable about some things and undependable about others. Could you become more dependable than you are?

Dependability through Time

Examples of dependability exist in history and literature:

- Wells Fargo was a transport company that started during the gold rush days in the American West. Miners who found gold had to ship it to other places to be valued. They counted on Wells Fargo's stagecoaches to help them out. Wells Fargo also transported passengers across the often-treacherous terrain. Eventually, Wells Fargo gained the reputation of being the best stagecoach line in the world.

- According to the Dutch story, Hans Brinker was a boy who lived in Haarlem, a city in Holland. His father was a sluicer, meaning that he opened and closed sluices, which are gates to canals. Opening these gates would release waters and keep the canals from overflowing. One day Hans came across a tiny leak in one of the sluices. This leak in the dike could cause disaster. He called for help, but nobody came. So Hans placed his finger in the dike, to stop the leak. He stayed all night despite cold and pain and weariness. Finally, the next morning somebody came along and got help for Hans.

Being dependable sometimes means you face danger and difficulty but still come through. Have you ever faced a challenge but done what you said you would? How did that make you feel? Would you do it again?

Being Dependable in Life

Consider this situation:

Wenda was delighted when she got on the community girls' softball team, but she was disappointed when team assignments were handed out. She was put in the outfield, where there was seldom much to do. Still, Wenda's mother told her she could watch and learn. Plus, she would get practice in hitting and fielding balls.

Wenda went to every practice all year long. She noticed others weren't as dependable. Sherri, the shortstop, often missed practices and occasionally a game. One day after practice, the coach stopped Wenda and thanked her for her work. "You never miss a practice or a game," he said. "And you stay in position and cover the outfield instead of running in to try to grab the ball from others. I can always depend on you. Thanks."

Wenda felt good about the compliments. However, she still wished she could get a chance at a more challenging position. In the fall, she got her chance. Sherri missed the last game of the season because her family was going to Disneyland. The coach went to Wenda and asked her to move into the shortstop position. Wenda agreed and caught the fly ball that changed the balance of the game. Her team won by 1 point.

People recognize those who are dependable. They may not jump in to grab the glory, but when the chips are down, they are the folks you turn to when you want to get things done. Can you think of the most dependable person in your life? Which person do you count on most?

Being Dependable in Practice

If somebody is counting on you for something, do everything you can to get it done. Don't make excuses or ignore your responsibilities. Focus on doing what you have promised. When you have done what you said you would, how do you feel? Being dependable puts some pressure on you to deliver, but it can also make you feel very good when you come through.

DEPENDABILITY CHECKLIST

○ If you promise something, deliver it.

○ Feel good about the fact that people can count on you.

○ Don't promise to do things you cannot do.

○ Find the resources you need to accomplish your goal.

○ Value the feeling you get when others believe in your ability to come through again and again.

Dependable Role Models

Here are people in various walks of life. Each has a reputation for being dependable.

- Cal Ripken, Jr., was a professional baseball player who did not miss a game for 14 years. Think about this: If you went from kindergarten through to your first year of college without missing a single day from school, you would be this dependable. Ripken broke the previous record for attendance held by Lou Gehrig. Ripken was the first player to win a Most Valuable Player Award, Major League Player of the Year Award, All Star MVP award, and Golden Glove, all in one season.

- Although he is a comedian, *Tonight Show* host Jay Leno is known as a hard worker who rarely takes time off. For more than 12 years, he never missed hosting a show until he and *Today Show* host Katie Couric exchanged their hosting duties once for publicity.

Dependable people may gain fame and fortune. Or they may live quiet lives in which they are appreciated but not given huge rewards for their dependability. As with all character traits, combining dependability with other traits such as courage or creativity can help you achieve amazing things.

What's in It for Me?

Consider these real-life consequences of being dependable:

- People admire you for getting the job done.

- At work, you may be rewarded with promotions and raises for doing what you promise.

- You gain more and more confidence in yourself because you always do what you say you will.

- Because people expect a lot of you, you must avoid overcommitting yourself.

Related Words to Explore

Here are some words related to the trait of being dependable and to its opposite:

- Reliable
- Trustworthy
- Staunch
- Resolute
- Loyal

- Faithful
- Steady
- Undependable
- Shifty

> **"**Resolve to perform what you ought; perform without fail what you resolve.**"**
> —Benjamin Franklin, Politician, Author, and Inventor

DETERMINED

To be determined means that you set your sights on a goal and don't let anything or anybody stop you. Determined people are not easily talked out of something. This trait can be great if the goal they are going after is a good one. It is not so great if they are determined to do something that is foolish or unwise. Still, many times others have said a course was foolish, and a determined person showed them to be wrong.

What are you determined about?

What Does It Mean to Be Determined?

Determined people may be able to achieve things others can't because they don't get discouraged. They have a goal, and they keep going to get to it. People may be determined to improve themselves in some way, fight for others, succeed at a job, or learn something new.

Talking determined people out of something is very difficult after they have decided to tackle it. If determined people keep after something long after it is practical to do so, they are seen as stubborn or foolish. Therefore, it's important that you combine your determination with wisdom about which goals are worth going after.

Have you ever been determined to do something? Did you succeed? What made you more determined about that goal than others?

Determination through Time

Efforts to go into outer space have shown great determination; for example:

- In 1957, Russia launched the first satellite sent into space, Sputnik. It was, in fact, the first manmade object ever to leave the earth's atmosphere. This launch was part of the International Geophysical year when both the United States and Russia said they would launch a satellite. Sputnik transmitted information using radio signals for three weeks before it burned up. The United States didn't launch its first satellite until 1958.

- President John F. Kennedy challenged this country to be the first to put a man on the moon. He made this challenge in a speech in 1961. In 1969, just eight years after Kennedy's speech, determined scientists, engineers, and astronauts landed the first person on the moon, proving how much determination can achieve.

Why are people determined to achieve certain things? They may do so for personal gain, to help others, or to do better than another person or country at something. The motive for your determination is important. If you are determined to do something not only for your own personal glory but for the good of others, are you a better person?

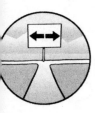

Being Determined in Life

Consider this situation:

Helena loved science. Her teacher told her about an international science fair competition that she thought Helena should try out for. She talked it over with her parents that night. Getting on the international team would take a lot of hard work. She would have to get some tutoring in chemistry to fill in where her classes left off. She also would have to work on weekends on a sample project to submit with the application.

Helena and her parents decided the effort was worthwhile, and she agreed the goal was important to her. She worked hard and her teacher thought she had a good chance of being picked. One Saturday, a letter arrived from the committee. Although Helena's application had been well received and the committee thought she had some great qualifications, they had had more applicants than ever before that year. Helena hadn't made the team.

The letter encouraged Helena to try again the next year. She went for a walk to think about her plans. That evening, Helena went to her parents and began to make plans for starting next year's project.

Can you set a goal and keep after it even if you are disappointed? Can you be determined about working hard and not stopping, no matter what? Determined people are hard to discourage. What are you most determined about in your life?

Being Determined in Practice

Perhaps there is something in your life you want very much. Maybe you want to win at a sport or learn to play the piano or ski. Pick something, and work very hard at it. Let your determination keep you going even when you are tired or feel defeated. What did you learn from your experience? Whether or not you achieved your goal, was your determination rewarding in some way?

DETERMINATION CHECKLIST

- ○ Set your sights on a goal, and go after it.
- ○ Don't let what others say discourage you.
- ○ Keep going even if you meet failure or difficulties.
- ○ Work hard, and put in the effort required to succeed.
- ○ Choose your goals wisely, and go after the things that really matter.
- ○ Enjoy the rewards you get when you reach your goals.

> **❝**Find a need and fill it.**❞**
> —Henry J. Kaiser, Industrialist

Determined Role Models

Here are people in various walks of life. Each has a reputation for being determined.

- William B. Travis was a lawyer and later became involved in the Texas Revolution, which fought against Mexican rule. The Texans took a fort called the Alamo, and Travis was sent there with reinforcements and eventually became commander. The small force was attacked, and those defending it were killed. The act of defending the Alamo helped to inspire the rest of Texas to fight to win independence. The determination of every person at the Alamo and especially their commander made them heroes in their countrymen's eyes.

- Casey Jones was a locomotive engineer in the late 1800s. He was dedicated to the railroad. A song tells of Jones's determination to always get the train to its destination. One day, after he had finished his work, he found out another man was sick and couldn't take his train out. On this rainy night, Casey came upon another train but did not have time to stop. Shouting at others to jump off the train to save themselves, Casey stayed at his post, pulling on the brakes and blowing the whistle.

- Shirin Ebadi is a champion of human rights in Iran. She won a Nobel Peace Prize in 2003, helping her to achieve even more in her fight against repression. Ebadi works for women's, children's, and workers' rights. Her determined fight against injustice has helped to bring hope to people in Iran.

What's in It for Me?

Consider these real-life consequences of being determined:

- People admire you for getting the job done.

- You seldom doubt your mission but keep going despite disappointment.

- Determined people often find ways to accomplish things others cannot because they won't be discouraged.

Related Words to Explore

Here are some words related to the trait of being determined and to its opposite:

- Dedicated
- Focused
- Strong-minded
- Resolute

- Firm
- Unwavering
- Changeable
- Irresolute

> **"**Paths clear before those who know where they're going and are determined to get there.**"**
> —**Anonymous**

DIGNIFIED

A dignified person has a sense of his or her own place in the world. Dignified people keep a calm, cool appearance even at difficult times. Sometimes dignified people are accused of being cold or condescending. However, truly dignified people expect other people to respect them as they respect others.

Do you know anybody you think of as dignified?

What Does It Mean to Be Dignified?

Dignity isn't confined to royalty. Everybody has the potential to be dignified, no matter what his or her job or position in life. Dignity consists of being gracious to everybody and acting graciously even when things go wrong.

Dignified people have an air about them. They seem to be polite and considerate to everybody they meet. They have a sense of their own position in the world. They never get upset by crises or problems around them. This calm self-confidence often provides an example that helps others get through crises. Dignified people can make good leaders.

Being dignified takes strength of character. It is more a strong sense of self than a specific action that you take. Have you ever acted in a dignified way?

Dignity through Time

Here are some examples of situations that required dignity:

- Surrendering in war is a difficult test of dignity. When one side wins, the other side must face failure with grace. During the Civil War, with the South's troops exhausted, General Robert E. Lee realized that he had no choice but to surrender to General Ulysses S. Grant. Both parties wanted a peaceful settlement. The surrender papers specified that the South's troops would lay aside their arms. But to spare Lee embarrassment, Grant added that officers would not be required to do so. As Lee rode away from the exchange, Grant and the Union soldiers saluted him in respect. Lee raised his hat in a dignified gesture and rode away to tell his troops the news of surrender.

- Some people feel that those who are dying should be allowed to do so with dignity. This is a difficult ethical situation. Throughout time, many people have been dignified when they came to the end of their lives.

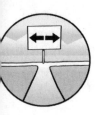

Being Dignified in Life

Consider this situation:

> *Mr. Peterson is a science teacher at Morrison Junior High. In one lesson, he said that metals conduct heat through the movement of the molecules in the metal.*
>
> *That night Josie mentioned to her father what Mr. Peterson had said. Josie's father, a scientist, told her Mr. Peterson was wrong. He said that it's not the molecules that conduct the heat. Instead, it's freely moving electrons (smaller pieces that make up molecules) that do so.*
>
> *After Mr. Peterson took attendance in class the next day, Josie stood up and told him what her father had said. He looked at her thoughtfully and then asked the class to come over to the computer. He performed a search for information about how metals conduct heat. He read out loud some sentences from a few articles and then turned to the assembled students.*
>
> *"Josie is right," he said. "I was wrong. Thank you, Josie, for bringing the correct information back to the class."*

Mr. Peterson could have been angry when Josie said he was wrong. He could have told her it was she who was wrong. He could have let the class go on thinking that what he had taught them was true. Instead, he showed dignity in checking the facts on the spot and admitting his error. He also praised Josie. Would you have shown as much dignity if someone accused you of being wrong?

Being Dignified in Practice

The next time you make a mistake or lose at something, try to act in a dignified way. Keep your sense of self-respect and don't overreact. If you lose a game, congratulate the winner and mean it. If you've made a mistake, admit it. Then move on, and learn from your mistake. Keep a check on your emotions, and don't let a problem overwhelm you. Act graciously to everybody involved.

DIGNITY CHECKLIST

- ⬭ Maintain a sense of your own worth even when you are going through difficult times.
- ⬭ Respect all people, and expect them to respect you.
- ⬭ Show a calm, controlled demeanor to others even in challenging moments.
- ⬭ Learn to control your emotions in front of others.
- ⬭ Never take unfair advantage of your position or power.

Dignified Role Models

Here are people who have a reputation for being dignified:

- Grace Kelly was born to a wealthy family in Philadelphia. As a young woman, she became a successful actress in movies. She met Prince Rainier of Monaco while filming a movie in his country, and they eventually married. After she became a princess, Grace supported many worthy causes in her adopted country. Although she had less freedom in her royal life than she had had in her film career, she always behaved as a princess with dignity and self-respect.

- John Jacob Astor was the great grandson of a German immigrant to America who made his fortune in fur trading. Astor dabbled in inventions and real estate. He volunteered as a staff colonel in the Spanish American War. Perhaps his most dignified moment came when he was a passenger on the doomed Titanic. After the ship hit an iceberg, he asked whether he could accompany his pregnant wife in a lifeboat. When he was reminded that women and children would have to go first, he accepted the situation with dignity. He gave his wife his gloves to keep her hands warm and remained on deck, where he went down with the ship.

To be aware of your responsibilities and be thoughtful about how you shoulder them is part of dignity. When you are under stress, will you panic or remain calm? Will you show respect for yourself and others and act according to your conscience? Dignity is not easy to maintain, but it is always recognized and respected.

What's in It for Me?

Dignified people can reap many benefits. For example, they can

- Rise above failure and ridicule because they always feel worthy of respect.

- Show others by their example how to rise above adversity.

- Be respected by others for their calmness under stress.

- Be rewarded in their careers by being placed in positions of leadership.

Related Words to Explore

Here are some words related to the trait of being dignified and to its opposite:

- Distinguished
- Decorous
- Stately
- Noble
- Classy

- Gracious
- Undignified
- Crass
- Rude

> **"**No race can prosper till it learns that there is as much dignity in tilling a field as in writing a poem.**"**
> —**Booker T. Washington, Educator**

FAIR

Being fair means being able to put aside your own feelings and prejudices. Fair people are impartial. They do not assume anything until they hear all the facts. They listen to those facts and then decide the right course of action.

Because everyone has opinions and prejudices, being fair and impartial is not easy. You have to try to imagine other people's feelings and views and put aside your own.

Do you think you know how to be fair?

What Does It Mean to Be Fair?

Fairness involves weighing the public good against the individual good. It means looking at what is right above what you, as a person, want. Being fair means putting aside the things you believe in and trying to understand what others believe.

Fairness is involved when a judge makes a decision in a court of law. However, what is considered fair under the law varies from one culture to another. Fairness is based on the culture and the ideas of the time. So, being fair involves understanding the values of society as well as being impartial.

Fairness through Time

Fairness is a trait that often appears in fairy tales:

- In *Rumpelstiltskin* by the Brothers Grimm, a man brags to the king that his daughter can spin gold from straw. A mysterious man appears before the girl and promises to produce the gold in exchange for gifts. The final gift he wants is her first-born child if she becomes queen. In desperation, she promises to give him the child. Later, after this new queen has a child, he says if she can guess his name, she can keep the child. She sends a messenger to learn all the names in the kingdom. The messenger overhears Rumpelstiltskin singing his name in the woods. He tells the queen the name Rumpelstiltskin. She gets to keep the child.

- In Hans Christian Andersen's story *The Princess and the Pea*, a woman arrives at a castle claiming to be a princess. Before the prince will marry her, she must prove she is a princess. The prince's mother tries a test. She places a pea under 20 mattresses to see whether the princess is sensitive enough to sense the pea as she sleeps. The next morning the princess awakes after having slept badly. She not only felt the single pea, but also had bruises from having slept on it.

Is it fair that the queen in the first story guesses Rumpelstiltskin's name after sending someone to overhear him? What about the bargain—was it unfair to begin with? In the second story, is the pea under the mattresses a fair test of a royal nature? Who should determine what test to give people and what it takes to pass a test?

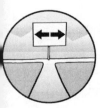

Being Fair in Life

Consider this situation:

Andrea and Michelle used to be friends, but over the summer they had an argument about a boy they both liked. Ever since the school year began, Andrea had been doing mean things to Michelle. She called her names and said bad things about her to the other girls in her class. Once she knocked Michelle's books out of her arms in the hallway, claiming it was an accident. One day in class while working on art projects, Andrea spilled some paint on Michelle's picture. Michelle had had enough, and she slapped Andrea.

The teacher came over and told Michelle to go to the principal's office. In tears, Michelle explained that Andrea had been picking on her all year long. The teacher said he didn't care why she had done it and sent her out of class.

Was it fair that Michelle ended up being punished even though Andrea was the cause of the fight? Was it fair that the teacher didn't listen to the whole story? If the teacher only saw Michelle slapping Andrea but didn't see Andrea spill paint on Michelle's picture, could he make a fair decision?

> **❝**We must be trusted to always place the public's good above our own and to always choose fairness over favoritism.**❞**
>
> —M. Jodi Rell, Governor

Being Fair in Practice

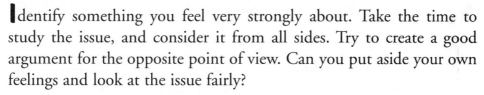

Identify something you feel very strongly about. Take the time to study the issue, and consider it from all sides. Try to create a good argument for the opposite point of view. Can you put aside your own feelings and look at the issue fairly?

If you can consider a difficult issue from various sides, you have it in you to show fairness. Can you avoid jumping to conclusions? Can you admit that you may not know everything and suspend your judgment until all the facts are in?

FAIRNESS CHECKLIST

- ◯ Learn to be objective about issues.
- ◯ Put aside your own feelings to try to understand the feelings of others.
- ◯ See various sides of a question before coming to a conclusion.
- ◯ Focus on what is fair, not on what people will think of your decision.
- ◯ Consider the greater good of the community over your own good or the good of any individual.
- ◯ Be willing to change your mind.
- ◯ Never jump to conclusions.

Fair Role Models

Here are people from various walks of life. Each has a reputation for fairness.

- Oliver Wendell Holmes, Jr., was a judge on the United States Supreme Court. His reputation for fairness is built on the fact that he put aside outworn customs to look at issues in light of changes in modern society. He believed law should change as society changes. He also supported a philosophy of "judicial restraint," which states that a judge should put aside personal opinions when making a decision in court.

- Justice Sandra Day O'Connor had a difficult road to the Supreme Court. After she graduated third in her class at Stanford Law School in 1950, the only job offers she received were for legal secretary positions. O'Connor then started her own law office and was appointed as a judge in Arizona. Her time on the Supreme Court was been marked by unpredictability: Those who thought they knew which way she would vote on any decision have been surprised when she made each decision on the case's merits. She seemed uniquely able to put aside her personal and political associations and made decisions based on the facts.

Fairness is crucial to judges. But fairness for a judge is based on the law. If a law itself is unfair, until it is changed, a judge has to enforce it. What is fair changes over time. Once it was considered fair that women and black people could not vote in America. Now that is considered unfair, and the law has changed.

What's in It for Me?

Consider these real-life consequences of being fair:

- You will gain the respect of others.

- You may be chosen to be a judge, either in the legal system or in a competition or contest.

- If you are a manager, your employees will appreciate your fairness.

- You learn to see both sides of a question, which makes you a more open-minded person.

Related Words to Explore

Here are some words related to the trait of being fair and to its opposite:

- Just
- Even-handed
- Reasonable
- Impartial
- Rational
- Nondiscriminatory
- Biased
- Unjust

FOCUSED

People who are focused can concentrate on one thing at a time or one goal. They are not distracted by people or activities around them. They can keep their attention on one outcome and do everything that's required to get there.

In what ways are you focused?

What Does It Mean to Be Focused?

Some people have difficulty focusing their attention on the task at hand or even on a long-term goal. The ability to concentrate and put your energy toward one thing is the ability to focus. Focus can be very useful in life. Being able to focus means that you can concentrate on something until you succeed.

Some people focus on goals with an intensity that is impressive. They are not confused or put off by other issues. People who play sports or perform in dance, music, or theater can put aside the distractions of hundreds of people in an audience and focus on their performances.

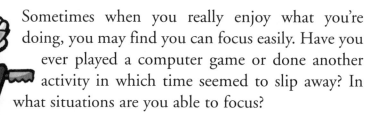

Sometimes when you really enjoy what you're doing, you may find you can focus easily. Have you ever played a computer game or done another activity in which time seemed to slip away? In what situations are you able to focus?

Focus through Time

Here examples of focus in occupations:

- People who cut diamonds need to make a single cut count. They are entrusted with thousands of dollars every time they cut into a stone. If they cut the stone badly, a lot of money can be lost. If they cut it well, they are rewarded and a beautiful thing is created for eternity. Every stone is different, with the weight of the stone distributed differently. Diamond cutters must focus to find the best cut to disperse light through the diamond in the most attractive way. And they get only one chance to do it.

- If you walk a tightrope, you need to know how to focus. If you have ever been to a circus, you have seen people balancing far above the ground on tightropes. If these people lose focus, they could fall. Tightrope walkers practice and plan their acts. Yet the concentration and focus they find when actually walking the tightrope are key to their success and their survival.

Many people do not have such high stakes when performing a job. We may not spend our days cutting diamonds or walking tightropes. Still, the same focus on the work at hand can help people overcome obstacles. If you enjoy something and want to become better at it, consider improving your focus on the task before you.

> **❝**Productivity is never an accident. It is always the result of a commitment to excellence, intelligent planning, and focused effort.**❞**
>
> **—Paul Meyer, Sports Journalist**

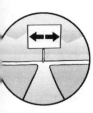

Being Focused in Life

Consider this situation:

Andrea had been studying ballet since she was four years old. She practiced an hour every day and took three hours of classes a week.

When her ballet teacher announced that the class would perform at a regional competition, Andrea decided she would do the very best job she could. She began to practice two hours every day and take four hours of classes a week.

When the competition came, Andrea felt ready. She went on stage and became totally focused on her performance. She wasn't aware of the audience or her teacher standing in the wings of the theater. She focused entirely on her dance and partners.

Certain activities require complete concentration for you to be successful. But no matter what your task or work, focus will help you do a better job.

Being Focused in Practice

Think of something you want to achieve and focus on it. Find ways to give yourself the time and quiet to work on your goal.

Do you find that trying to focus helps you make progress on your goal?

FOCUS CHECKLIST

○ Pick a time and place that allow you to focus.

○ Find a goal you can put your energy toward.

○ Don't let those around you distract you from your goal.

○ Create a space that is uncluttered and quiet. Make sure it allows you to focus your attention on your work.

Focused Role Models

Here are people with a reputation for being focused.

- Michelle Kwan is a professional ice skater. When she is training, she has three 45-minute practice sessions on ice with her coach. She also does an hour workout in a gym, some weight training, and runs more than 3½ miles a day. Her focus has paid off: She is the most decorated figure skater in the United States. Kwan has won 42 championships. Figure skating requires practice, but equally important is the focus required when performing routines on the ice in front of thousands of people.

- Ludwig van Beethoven found his original fame as a concert pianist. Although he did compose in those years, he was most rewarded for his performing. He actually disliked performing, so he gradually developed the ability to forget the audience and focus on his playing. When he began losing his hearing, he had to change his focus to composing. As his hearing faded, he had to hold his head on the piano to hear the notes he was composing in his head. The concentration and effort this required are impressive.

> **"**Only when your consciousness is totally focused on the moment you are in can you receive whatever gift, lesson, or delight that moment has to offer. **"**
> —Barbara De Angelis, Psychologist and Author

What's in It for Me?

Consider these real-life consequences of being focused:

- You can become an expert in one or more areas.

- People respect your ability to master a particular task or skill.

- You are not easily distracted by things and people around you.

- You may achieve great things because you can focus on your goals.

Related Words to Explore

Here are some words related to the trait of being focused and to its opposite:

- Alert
- Paying attention
- Concentrating
- Determined

- Driven
- Inattentive
- Scattered
- Unfocused

FORGIVING

Although you can tell people you forgive them for something they have done, really forgiving means that you don't hold any bad feelings and don't lay blame. You tend to look forward more than you focus on the problems of the past. Being forgiving isn't always easy. You have to put aside feelings of frustration, anger, and resentment. You have to truly find it in your heart to excuse a fault or offense.

Have you been in situations in which it was hard to forgive somebody? What would forgiving that person have felt like? What would it have cost you?

What Does It Mean to Be Forgiving?

Forgiving is admitting that a person has committed an offense of some kind but also admitting that you can forget it. You look beyond the person's actions and continue to see the value of the person. You realize everybody makes mistakes and you are also not perfect. Forgiving involves an understanding that nobody can be good or right all the time.

Consider the alternative to forgiving. Instead of forgiving, you may hold a grudge. You may never speak to the person again. Usually, being unable to forgive somebody causes more harm than good. Have you ever refused to forgive somebody? How did that feel? Did you lose a friend or feel uncomfortable every time you saw that person?

Forgiveness through Time

There are examples of forgiveness in history. Here are two:

- Sometimes illegal immigrants enter countries. They are breaking the law. However, they often become good, law-abiding citizens. Occasionally, countries grant amnesty for illegal immigrants. Amnesty is a way to forgive a whole group of people. After providing amnesty, countries allow people who have lived there a long time to stay in the country legally. The act of entering the country may have been wrong, but since that time, these people have been productive and contributed to the country. So, they are forgiven.

- After World War II, the United States occupied Japan. Though these two countries fought against each other throughout the war, when America won, it did not take revenge. One reason for this forgiveness was the new Cold War with Russia: America wanted to show Asian countries that democracy was the best system, rather than the communism of the Soviet Union. Americans provided food and relief to the defeated people.

> **"**Forgiveness is a gift of high value. Yet its cost is nothing.**"**
>
> —Betty Smith, Dramatist

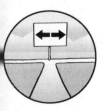

Being Forgiving in Life

Consider this situation:

Andy had asked his friend Mark to come over and help him fix his bike. Mark had a tool that Andy needed to do the repair. By 5:15 when Mark hadn't shown up, Andy was getting angry. He'd hoped to ride his bike to school in the morning, and if Mark didn't show, he couldn't fix the bike tonight.

By 5:30 Andy was pacing around the backyard, angrier by the minute. You don't just break a promise, he thought. He went inside and phoned Mark's house. His mother told him that Mark had gone out to the movies.

The next day Andy went to school by bus. He was still fuming that Mark not only forgot about helping him, but didn't call to apologize. As he got off the bus, Mark walked up to him.

"Hey," he said, "my mom said you called last night. It was a three-hour movie, so I got in really late. That's why I didn't call you back. So, what's up? Are we still on for working on your bike tonight?"

Obviously, Mark had simply mixed up the days. If you were Andy, what would you do? Would you yell at your friend, remind him of the promise he'd broken, or let go of your anger and just forget about it? It's natural to want to release your anger, but are there times it's not worthwhile to do that?

Being Forgiving in Practice

Look for a situation in which somebody in your life needs forgiveness. If somebody makes a mistake or does something wrong, consider telling that person it's okay rather than making him or her feel bad about it. Reassure that person that we all make mistakes and it's better to focus on how to fix the problem than on who caused it or how it happened. Then help the person to make things right.

Did you find that you were able to let go of blame and focus on the person rather than the mistake? If you did, you have shown true forgiveness.

FORGIVENESS CHECKLIST

○ Don't focus on blame.

○ Understand that everybody makes mistakes.

○ Help others to recover from the consequences of their mistakes.

○ Look to the future instead of the past.

○ Admit that nobody's perfect—even you.

Forgiving Role Models

Here are some people who have a reputation for forgiveness:

- Jimmy Carter, President of the United States following the Vietnam War, had campaigned on a promise to grant a pardon to people who had avoided the draft during the Vietnam War. During the war, many people left the country or did not register for the draft. Such draft dodging was illegal, and the country could have prosecuted these people. He showed forgiveness in an effort to heal a wound in American society so that everybody could move forward.

- Bishop Desmond Tutu trained as a teacher and then studied theology. He has fought for a just society in South Africa that doesn't discriminate among races. He worked to end apartheid, a policy separating blacks and whites in his country. Despite many years of oppression of black people by whites, he has shown a very forgiving attitude that focuses on making a better future and leaving behind differences of the past.

> **❝**Forgiveness is the act of admitting we are like other people.**❞**
> —Christina Baldwin, Dramatist

What's in It for Me?

Consider these real-life consequences of being forgiving:

- You do not pressure others into feeling bad about their mistakes, which makes you more likeable.

- You are not too hard on yourself when you make mistakes.

- People tend to trust you because they know you will not act harshly if they make an error.

- You are viewed as fair and tolerant of others' weaknesses.

Related Words to Explore

Here are some words related to forgiving and to its opposite:

- Merciful
- Pardoning
- Lenient
- Forbearing
- Magnanimous
- Sympathetic

- Tolerant
- Indulgent
- Unforgiving
- Hard-hearted
- Intolerant

GENEROUS

Being generous means giving freely to others. Generous people might give money to a charity or pay to buy pizza for everybody working on a project with them. They might give their time to other people to help them out. They could be generous in showing their affection or support for somebody who needs it.

In what ways are you a generous person?

What Does It Mean to Be Generous?

Generous people are not those who give money to get a tax credit or to make people like them. Truly generous people care about others and feel that everyone has an obligation to share. Sometimes generous people have been helped by others. In turn, they want to repay or pass on that generosity.

A generous nature can be revealed in many ways. If you have no money to give others, do you give in other ways? Do you consider what the other person needs more often than you think about your own needs? Do you feel rewarded by the act of giving, even if nobody knows that you gave?

If you like to give things to others whether or not you get something back, you may be a naturally generous person.

Generosity through Time

Nations and organizations have been generous to others in difficult times, for example:

- Many countries send help in the form of money or materials to other countries when natural disasters hit. The Red Cross is an organization with chapters all over the world. It was originally dedicated to providing help to victims of war. The International Committee of the Red Cross was begun in Switzerland in 1863 to help those victims with donations of blood, materials, and money. Over the years, the organization has broadened its goals to include providing help to victims of all kinds of disasters.

- When terrorists attacked the World Trade Center in New York City on September 11, 2001, the United States didn't need money or doctors. What could other countries do to help? Many countries gave in the form of a generous outpouring of sympathy and support. People held rallies and candlelight prayer meetings for the victims. Tributes of flowers appeared at American embassies in major cities around the world. That generosity of spirit from around the world did a lot to comfort the American people and families of victims.

You can be generous in various ways. Money is only one way to show your generosity. You can also give your time, your skills, or your love to help others. A generous businessperson, for example, might not only give money to charity, but also give her time to help a young person get started in business. How have you been generous in your life?

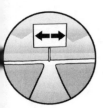

Being Generous in Life

Consider this situation:

Rachel had been at the mall for about an hour when she saw Carlos sitting in the food court. He was in her class, but Rachel didn't know him well. She had heard that Carlos' mother had died a week before. Everybody felt really sorry for him, of course. However, Rachel hadn't thought whether she could do something to help until she saw him sitting there alone.

Taking out her wallet, Rachel counted her money. There was just enough for her to buy the burger she was hungry for. Suddenly, she made a decision. She went to the cookie shop, paid for a giant cookie, and took it over to Carlos. "Here," she said. "Thought you could use something to eat." He looked up at her and then at the cookie. "Thanks," he said. Even though she had only a half hour before her mother was supposed to pick her up, Rachel sat down and asked Carlos if he needed to talk about his mom. With tears in his eyes, he started talking about how he felt. After a few minutes, he seemed to calm down and then thanked Rachel for stopping.

How was Rachel generous to Carlos? Did spending the few dollars on the cookie make her generous? Do you have to give a lot to make a difference? Would you have stopped to talk to Carlos?

Being Generous in Practice

Spend some time thinking about the people around you and what they need from you. Would buying an ice cream cone for a friend who is sad cheer him up? Would loaning somebody your bike to run an errand make a difference to her? Could you give your time to help somebody talk over a problem or finish a project? Try giving people things they need for one day. Was it hard to do? Was it rewarding?

GENEROSITY CHECKLIST

○ Don't be stingy with money.

○ Give your time and caring to people in need.

○ Don't spend more time thinking about yourself than you do about others.

○ If you have been successful at something, think about what you can give back to the people who helped you succeed.

○ Be willing to give to others even in situations in which you might have to deprive yourself in some way.

"*That's what I consider true generosity. You give your all, and yet you always feel as if it costs you nothing.***"**
—Simone de Beauvoir, Author

Generous Role Models

Here are people who have a reputation for being generous:

- Andrew Carnegie was at one time the richest man in the world. He made his money in the steel industry. Because he believed that rich people have a moral obligation to give some money back to society, he founded the Carnegie Institute. One of the causes that Carnegie supported was the creation of libraries all around America. One of the reasons for Carnegie's generosity was another act of generosity. When he was a little boy, a rich man in his town allowed local boys to use his library free, no matter how poor their families were.

- Bill and Melinda Gates donated more than $3 billion to charities in 2004. As founder of Microsoft Corporation, Bill Gates has become very wealthy. The Bill and Melinda Gates Foundation gives money to support improved learning and health care.

- Madam C.J. Walker was born in 1867 to former slaves. She developed a hair conditioning treatment that she sold door to door. Over time, she made a fortune from her cosmetics. She became one of the most successful businesspeople of her time. She gave generously to black charities of the time. She funded scholarships at universities.

Well-known philanthropists are typically wealthy people who feel that they should give back to the world that supported their success. However, anybody can practice philanthropy, which is giving to support causes and charities. You can give any amount of time or money. Are there causes you would like to give to? If you don't have money, could you give your time or skills instead?

What's in It for Me?

Consider these real-life consequences of being generous:

- You are seen as a kind person.

- You can witness the results of your generosity in the improvement of a person or your community.

- You understand the value of things more important than money.

- If you have been generous in the past, when you need help, people are more likely to be generous to you.

- You can feel good about the people you have helped.

Related Words to Explore

Here are some words related to the trait of being generous and to its opposite:

- Bighearted
- Munificent
- Giving
- Philanthropic
- Liberal

- Greedy
- Tightfisted
- Stingy
- Ungiving

> **"**Generosity with strings is not generosity. It is a deal. **"**
> —Marya Mannes, Writer

GENTLE

Gentle people do not like violence. Instead, they tend to treat others with kindness and care. They don't do things by force, but typically have a more quiet, friendly way of getting things done.

Do you know people who are gentle?

What Does It Mean to Be Gentle?

There are many examples of people who have used peaceful, nonviolent means to make change in the world. Instead of using force, they communicate with others or lead by quiet example. Gentle people are not necessarily weak. Indeed, they may have great strength and courage. However, the means they use to get things done involves cooperation and caring.

People who can be gentle with other people or animals may become healers or ministers. They handle others' feelings with kindness. Gentle people may have a calming influence on others. When people are treated with gentleness, they often become more gentle in return.

Is a part of you gentle? Do you treat little children or pets gently? Do you treat yourself or your friends with gentleness? When you are gentle instead of angry, how do people treat you?

Gentleness through Time

Here are examples of gentleness among groups of people:

- Vegetarians believe it is wrong to kill animals for meat. These people eat vegetables, fruits, grains, and nuts, but never meat. They think that animals have rights just like people. Often vegetarians work for the humane treatment of animals. Vegetarians don't think that human life is more important than animal life.

- Pacifists believe that fighting is wrong. Pacifists oppose the use of force to settle a disagreement among people. They feel there is a better way to solve differences. Although some people believe war is justifiable in certain circumstances, violence is never the answer to a pacifist.

People who use peaceful means to make change may have to endure violence from less gentle people. Do you have the courage to take a stand without using force?

> **"**Like water, be gentle and strong. Be gentle enough to follow the natural paths of the earth, and strong enough to rise up and reshape the world.**"**
> —Brenda Peterson, Nature Writer

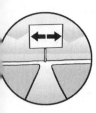

Being Gentle in Life

Consider this situation:

Being the new kid at the school was tough. Everybody seemed to pick on Ian. One boy in particular, Jack, was a bully and tried to pick a fight with Ian every day.

Ian refused to fight, but one day Jack knocked him down. Ian picked himself up and started to walk away, which made Jack angrier. Jack challenged Ian to a fight on Saturday. Ian said he bet Jack was a good pool player and challenged him to a game at the community center. On Saturday, the two boys played a game, with several of their friends looking on. Jack won. Ian congratulated Jack, and Jack bragged all day about how he'd won. After that, Jack and Ian became friends.

Did Jack realize that Ian had used his brains to avoid violence? Ian gave Jack an opportunity to win, which Jack liked to do, but in a nonviolent way. Can you be gentle when someone else is not?

> **"**When you encounter difficulties and contradictions, do not try to break them, but bend them with gentleness and time.**"**
> —Saint Francis de Sales

Young Person's Character Education Handbook, © JIST Life

Being Gentle in Practice

The next time you are in a situation of conflict, a situation in which there is disagreement and people are getting upset, try using gentleness instead of anger. How did the other people involved react? Did you feel your own calmness helped others to calm down?

GENTLENESS CHECKLIST

- ◯ Use words and your intelligence to solve problems.
- ◯ Treat other creatures with tenderness.
- ◯ Avoid getting angry when something upsetting happens.
- ◯ Avoid the use of force.

> **"**Criticism, like rain, should be gentle enough to nourish a man's growth without destroying his roots.**"**
> —Frank A. Clark, Writer

Gentle Role Models

Here are two people who were at the center of religious movements. Each has a reputation for gentleness.

- Jesus Christ preached about a loving, forgiving god. One of the 10 commandments at the core of Christianity forbids people to kill. Another basic belief from Christ was that if somebody hurts you, you should not retaliate. All accounts of the day speak of Jesus as a gentle person who preached against violence.

- Buddha is the name given to Siddhartha Gautama, a prince in what is today India. Buddha was troubled by the suffering he saw around him. His teachings say that we should lose our attachment to possessions to free us from suffering. Every Buddhist monk takes a vow that he will not kill any living thing, even an insect, because life is sacred.

Many religions have at their center a belief in nonviolence and respect for other people. Whether or not you support a formal religion, you may want to use their ideas as a model for gentleness.

> **"**Only the weak are cruel. Gentleness can only be expected from the strong.**"**
> —Leo Buscaglia, Writer

What's in It for Me?

Consider these real-life consequences of being gentle:

- Gentle people help resolve situations without violence and are seen as peacekeepers.

- When you treat people gently, they will often treat you gently, as well.

- In work situations, gentle people are often admired for their ability to calmly work through problems without getting angry or emotional.

- Gentle people may find rewarding work in careers in which they can solve problems peacefully or take care of others.

Related Words to Explore

Here are some words related to the trait of being gentle and to its opposite:

- Mild
- Calm
- Kind
- Tender
- Caring

- Peaceful
- Rough
- Abrasive
- Violent

GOOD CITIZEN

Ask two people what makes a good citizen, and you may get different answers. Some believe a good citizen is one who follows the rules made by society. Others think a good citizen is one who focuses on the good of the community above his or her own welfare. Still others consider people good citizens if they fight to change unjust laws or intolerant views. What do you think makes a good citizen?

What Does It Mean to Be a Good Citizen?

Though we are becoming a more global society, the world is still broken into groups. There are communities, states or provinces, countries, and collectives of countries, such as the European Union. To keep order, groups have created rules and standards, often in the form of laws. Laws try to stop people from stealing or breaking promises to each other, for example.

Good citizens support what's best for the larger group. For that reason, they typically uphold laws. However, laws are not always right. What worked 100 years ago may not work today. For example, 100 years ago, black people were prevented from voting in America. Today, they are able to vote because a law was changed. The people who worked to change this law saw a way to make society stronger.

Good citizens may work for the community's good by volunteering or becoming politicians. Being a good citizen can be as simple as voting in elections. Everyone can be a good citizen by being aware of society's issues and participating in the community.

Good Citizenship through Time

There are many examples of good citizenship. Here are two, one from history and one from the movies:

- The Boston Tea Party happened shortly before the American Revolution. In Boston Harbor, American patriots boarded a ship that had transported tea from England. Because the British had levied a heavy tax on tea, Americans felt they were being treated unfairly. They threw the tea overboard to protest the tax. Eventually, a war was fought to free America from British rule. But that night in Boston when a group fought for change is an interesting example of working for the good of the group. Of course, the British saw this vandalism as bad citizenship!

- In the movie *Mr. Smith Goes to Washington*, a man is appointed to the United States Congress. When he finds out that his appointment was arranged by a dishonest man, he tries to tell the people of his state about the dishonesty. He starts a filibuster, which allows a senator to hold the floor for as long as he wishes. Though tired and feeling defeated, Mr. Smith continues to speak about the dishonesty in his state until he finally gets the support of the people and wins his fight.

Being a good citizen involves acting for the common good. That good may be in upholding laws or in fighting for change. Do you see things in your community that you want to support? Are there other things that could use your efforts to make the place you live better?

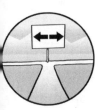

Being a Good Citizen in Life

Consider this situation:

> *Josh stopped Shireen in the hallway one afternoon. He asked her if she'd be willing to run for student council with him. He was campaigning to be president, and he needed a vice president on his ticket. Shireen was the smartest girl in the class, he said, and he wanted her to run with him. He had some ideas about changing the system that would help kids get heard about important issues.*
>
> *Shireen liked Josh and was flattered. She didn't want to hurt his feelings, but she had so much to do right now, what with her music lessons and a recital in a few months. She considered the much-needed changes Josh had proposed and thought for another few seconds. Could she make a difference? Then she gave him his answer.*

Have you ever been too busy to do something for a group you live in, whether that group is your family, your community, or your country? Should everybody make time in his or her life for public service of some kind? Do you think you can be a good citizen even if you don't get involved in politics?

> **❝** Never doubt that a small group of thoughtful, committed citizens can change the world. Indeed, it is the only thing that ever has. **❞**
>
> —**Margaret Mead, Anthropologist**

Being a Good Citizen in Practice

Read your local paper and identify a public issue that you feel strongly about. Perhaps a local business is polluting the environment. Maybe a group is fighting to fund a local arts center or shelter for homeless people. Try to identify a few ways that you could help. Could you campaign to get people to vote on the issue? Could you volunteer to support a group working for change? Could you change the way you do things (for example, riding your bike more often than riding in a car to help protect the environment). Try taking steps to work for your community's good.

What was the result of your efforts? Did you encounter support or resistance? How did you feel afterward? Do you feel you made a difference?

GOOD CITIZENSHIP CHECKLIST

◯ Think of the good of the larger group ahead of yourself.

◯ Consider whether current rules and values are fair to the entire group.

◯ Actively work to improve the conditions of your community.

◯ Listen to the concerns of others to understand the needs of the larger community.

◯ Participate: Vote, turn out for public discussions, and take action to make positive change.

Good Citizen Role Models

Here are some people who have a reputation for good citizenship:

- Golda Meir was the Prime Minister of Israel for five years. Prior to that, as Foreign Minister of Israel, she worked on cooperative agriculture plans between Israel and Africa. As Labor Minister, she worked for the people of Israel. She worked for the protection of European Jews during World War II. In 1948, she belonged to the People's Council, which signed the proclamation establishing the state of Israel. She was dedicated to her country and was known for her deep caring for all people in the world.

- Thabo Mbeki, President of South Africa, has worked hard, not only for his own country, but for the greater good of all African nations. He has been involved in trying to bring peace to Burundi, which is undergoing a civil war. He has worked to fight war and disease in the Congo. As a praised peacemaker, Mbeki has acted in the greater interests of his continent as well as his country.

- Susan B. Anthony worked for causes related to women's rights in the late nineteenth and early twentieth centuries, including the right of women to vote. She took a group of women to a voting station as a protest and was arrested. She campaigned for an amendment to the constitution. She organized the International Council of Women and the International Suffrage Alliance, which worked for women's rights worldwide. She worked tirelessly for the greater good of her gender, her country, and her world.

What's in It for Me?

Consider these real-life consequences of being a good citizen:

- You can have an impact on your world that may make other people's lives better.

- You may improve the conditions under which you and others live.

- You gain the respect of others.

- You may participate in historical change.

Related Words to Explore

Here are some words related to the trait of being a good citizen and to its opposite:

- Nationalistic
- Involved
- Active
- Revolutionary

- Supportive
- Uninvolved
- Passive
- Apathetic

> **"***And so, my fellow Americans, ask not what your country can do for you. Ask what you can do for your country. My fellow citizens of the world, ask not what America will do for you, but what together we can do for the freedom of man.* **"**
>
> **—John F. Kennedy, U.S. President**

HARD WORKING

Hard-working people would rather be busy than sit in front of a television set or relax on the beach. They find rewards in their work and can't imagine being too idle. People who work hard achieve a great deal in life. They often take on many more chores than others.

Here's a common saying: If you want to find somebody who can help, find somebody who is busy. What do you think that means?

What Does It Mean to Be Hard Working?

One trick to becoming hard working is to find work that you enjoy. Then the work is not difficult and the act of work is rewarding. People who hate what they do for a living may find it very difficult to work hard.

People who work hard often get recognition for a job well done. They get bored if they don't work. Sometimes they are motivated by money, but often they are motivated by the pleasure work gives them and by accomplishment.

People who are hard working must guard against letting work become the only thing in their lives. They have to balance work with play and time spent with family and friends to have a happy life.

What kind of work do you like to do?

Hard Workers through Time

Hard work has produced many great buildings in our world, for example:

- The Empire State Building was started in 1930. Designed as the tallest building ever built to that date, it was constructed in only 14 months. The construction schedule was so aggressive that 4½ stories were completed every week. Seven million work hours were put in on the project by 3,400 workers working every day, including Sundays and holidays. The building was completed for half of its budgeted cost. It remains an impressive and beautiful building and a tribute to the hard work that made it possible.

- The pyramids in Giza, Egypt, were built over 20 or so years. Workers, both slaves and farmers who worked during their off season, were once thought to number about 100,000. Today, based on better knowledge of the time, it is believed that 2,000 or so men worked on the pyramids. These workers had to move 2.5-ton blocks of stone into place up the sides of the structures. Because of the building of the pyramids, Egyptians gained a reputation for being great builders.

People who are hired as part of a crew to complete work have to keep up with the expectations of their employers. Those who are not hard workers may lose their jobs. Some people make themselves work hard because they enjoy the work. Others work hard for rewards. What makes you feel like working hard?

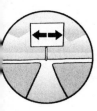

Being Hard Working in Life

Consider this situation:

Lanie and her sister Cherie were supposed to help their grandmother clean out the basement. They were going to take old things to the dump because they were moving in a month. Saturday morning, they went downstairs carrying some boxes to pack things in. They also took some garbage bags to throw away things they didn't need.

Lanie, Cherie, and their grandmother worked for about an hour, and then the phone rang. It was their friend Michelle asking if the two girls wanted to go to the mall. Cherie pleaded with her grandmother to let her go. Her grandmother looked at all the work left to do but reluctantly said okay.

Lanie didn't follow. "Aren't you going to the mall, too?" her grandmother asked.

"No," said Lanie. "I'd rather finish the work." She worked with her grandmother for four more hours. They laughed when they came across old stuff from Lanie's childhood. When they stopped, most of the basement was clean. She was tired, but she was glad she'd stayed. She had accomplished something. It made her happy.

Work isn't always fun, but it usually achieves something. Feeling good about getting something done is what hard work is all about. Would you have finished the work, or would you have gone to the mall? If working hard is its own reward for you, you have it in you to be a hard worker.

Being Hard Working in Practice

Pick one thing you would like to work toward, and set a schedule to complete it. Push yourself a little beyond what you think you can do. Put in time on the project each day, even if it's only an hour or two. When the project is finished, write down how you feel about what you've accomplished. What were the rewards of getting the work done? Did you do things you didn't think you could do? What was most difficult about putting in the extra work to get the project done? Would you do it again?

HARD-WORKING CHECKLIST

- ◯ Find work you enjoy, and then do it often.
- ◯ Appreciate the rewards you get from hard work.
- ◯ Don't overwork. Take the time to appreciate other things in life.
- ◯ Work at things that produce worthwhile results for your community.
- ◯ Avoid taking on work that isn't rewarding or interesting to you.

> **"**The secret of joy in work is contained in one word—excellence. To know how to do something well is to enjoy it. **"**
>
> —Pearl Buck, Novelist

Hard-Working Role Models

Here are people who have a reputation for being hard working:

- Pearl Buck was a writer and activist. She grew up in China, and many of her books are set in Asia. She wrote more than 80 works, including novels, plays, short stories, poems, children's books, and biographies. As a young woman, she worked in Asia as an interpreter and teacher and then obtained a master's degree in literature from Cornell. She was the first woman to win the Nobel Prize for literature. During World War II, she gave lectures on democracy. Buck was active in humanitarian causes like the East and West Foundation for mutual understanding between cultures. She was an advocate for women's and civil rights.

- Carl Sandburg was known as a poet, but he worked hard all his life in many jobs. He started working at age 13. He delivered milk, laid bricks, cut blocks of ice, threshed wheat, and shined shoes. When he grew up, he worked as a reporter and political activist. He wrote children's books, folk songs, a biography of Abraham Lincoln (for which he won the Pulitzer Prize), and books of poetry. He wrote of the gap between the rich and poor, having experienced poverty himself.

People who produce a great deal in their lives often get involved in many activities. Although they are often successful enough to stop working so hard, they get pleasure out of their work. Do you get a lot of pleasure from doing a particular type of work? Will you make it your life's work?

What's in It for Me?

Consider these real-life consequences of being hard working:

- You accomplish a great deal in your life.
- You may earn lots of money for the work you do.
- People admire you as somebody who gets things done.
- You are seldom bored.
- You may tackle things others don't, such as starting your own business.

Related Words to Explore

Here are some words related to the trait of being hard working and to its opposite:

- Diligent
- Industrious
- Thorough
- Capable
- Assiduous

- Energetic
- Workaholic
- Lazy
- Idle
- Couch Potato

> "The more I want to get something done, the less I call it work."
> —Richard Bach, Novelist

HELPFUL

Most of us cannot go through life without the help of others. We may need help with our schoolwork or on the job. People help us get through hard times or deal with problems. The world would be a much harder place if people didn't help each other.

In what ways are you helpful?

What Does It Mean to Be Helpful?

Most people are helpful at some time or another. People who help others on a regular basis might be described as helpful. Some help only those who are friends or family. Others help anybody in need. If a helpful person sees a stranger in trouble, he or she will immediately try to help.

Helpful people may have to make sacrifices to help others. They may think more about the welfare of others than their own. In life, helpful people may work in careers in which they can help others, for example, as teachers or nurses or psychiatrists.

Would you put aside thoughts of yourself to help a stranger? Do you try to help your friends and family when they need it? If you help others, they are more likely to help you when you need it.

Helpfulness through Time

Here are examples from history of people helping each other:

- During the bombing of London in World War II, Americans and Canadians opened their homes to child refugees and created aid packages. These relief efforts were assembled under an organization called the British War Relief Society. This organization took contributions of food and clothing from thousands of people. The American Theater Wing was a group of actresses who gave performances to benefit British war relief. Bundles for Britain gathered women together to knit garments for soldiers and civilians. These groups spent untold hours to help people they did not know.

- The Underground Railroad was a loosely organized group of people who opened their homes to runaway slaves prior to and during the American Civil War. Because they felt slavery was wrong, they put themselves in danger to help slaves escape. Abolitionists, those who wanted to see slavery abolished, helped people move from home to home across thousands of miles. At every moment, the runaway slaves were in danger of being recaptured. The only reward the abolitionists received was to know they had helped others gain freedom.

Helping others is a privilege. It allows us to feel we've made a difference. Helping people can be a way to act on our beliefs in a cause or moral issue. Have you ever helped somebody you never met? Why? How does helping people make you feel?

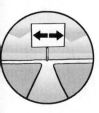

Being Helpful in Life

Consider this situation:

> *Nadia was the last to leave the school that day. She had stayed to help the substitute teacher clean up the room. As she approached the crosswalk, she noticed Mrs. Herrald standing next to a car. She was looking in the driver's window and appeared to be upset.*
>
> *Nadia could have crossed the road and continued home. Instead, she went over to Mrs. Herrald to see if she needed some help. Mrs. Herrald explained that the woman driving the car had stopped because she had become sick. "I think she might be having a heart attack," Mrs. Herrald said. Nadia told Mrs. Herrald to wait with the woman while she ran back into the school and got the principal to call an ambulance.*
>
> *When Nadia returned a few minutes later, paramedics were helping the woman. Mrs. Herrald seemed much calmer. "Thank you so much, Nadia, for your help. I don't know what I would have done if you hadn't come along."*

Opportunities to help people exist all around us. Some people ignore them or are too busy to help. Others go out of their way to help. Sometimes the effort is little, but the result is great. On your way to or from school today, look for an opportunity to help someone.

Young Person's Character Education Handbook, © JIST Life

Being Helpful in Practice

Check out local volunteer opportunities in your community. Identify one that helps people or animals or the environment. Then explore the possibility of helping out. Did you find an opportunity to help that would make you feel you were doing something worthwhile? Go ahead, give some of your time to make a difference!

HELPFULNESS CHECKLIST

◯ Look for opportunities to lend a hand.

◯ Join a group, or volunteer to help in an organized effort.

◯ Be willing to give up time or money you might have spent on yourself to help others.

◯ If somebody has a problem or is upset, ask if you can help.

◯ If somebody helps you, look for ways to repay him or her with help in the future.

> **❝**Refusing to ask for help when you need it is refusing someone the chance to be helpful.**❞**
> —**Ric Ocasek, Musician**

Helpful Role Models

Here are people with a reputation for being helpful.

- Hernando DeSoto is an economist from Peru who has studied the economies of poor societies for years. He has worked to get poor people legal title to their homes and businesses. That way, they can get credit and investment money to improve their conditions. He wants to help poor people to become a productive part of their societies.

- Dear Abby is a helpful advice column written by Abigail Van Buren, also known as Jeanne Phillips, and was founded by her mother, Pauline Phillips. It is the most popular and widely syndicated column in the world—known for its common sense and youthful perspective. Millions of people have written to Dear Abby seeking help and answers to their problems. The column is published in newspapers and online.

People can help each other by giving money, offering their support, or actually putting themselves in danger to protect others. Help can take many forms. Who are you in a position to help?

> **"**It is not helpful to help a friend by putting coins in his pockets when he has holes in his pockets.**"**
> —Elizabeth Bowen, Writer

What's in It for Me?

Consider these real-life consequences of being helpful:

- You are considered kind and caring by others.

- You may be able to make a difference in the world and turn around a bad situation for a group of people.

- Help is a two-way street: If you help others, they are more likely to help you.

- Employers appreciate helpful people who work as a team with their coworkers.

Related Words to Explore

Here are some words related to the trait of being helpful and to its opposite:

- Obliging
- Cooperative
- Supportive
- Team player

- Ready to lend a hand
- Unhelpful
- Obstructive
- Uninvolved

HONEST

Being honest means being truthful. We see examples of honesty and its opposite, dishonesty, all the time. In fact, most people tell lies about unimportant things. Some people make a habit of lying about important things. These people are considered dishonest.

Are you an honest person?

What Does It Mean to Be Honest?

Honesty is a complex character trait. Most of us don't honestly share everything we think and feel with everybody we meet, nor should we. Honesty without tact and caring can cause you to hurt people's feelings. Complete honesty may force you to share thoughts that you have a right to keep private. So when do you cross the line between telling acceptable lies and being dishonest?

Lying about things on a regular basis with the intent to deceive is a sign of a dishonest character. If people do not feel they can trust you because you often say one thing and do another, your relationships will suffer.

Honesty exists not only in the things you say, but also in the things you do. If you act differently than what you think or feel, you are being dishonest. The effect of your honesty on others may tell you how to act in any situation.

   Young Person's Character Education Handbook, © JIST Life

Honesty through Time

- A famous example of dishonesty is the Trojan horse. During the Trojan War, the Greeks held the city of Troy under siege. Their leader Odysseus got an idea about how to get into the city. He told his soldiers to build a large wooden horse. The statue was large enough for soldiers to hide inside. After they did, the fleet sailed away. The people of Troy came out to look at the horse. Against the protests of a couple of people, they dragged the horse into the city. That night, while people slept or celebrated their victory, the Greek soldiers crept out of the horse. They killed the citizens of Troy.

- Mahatma Gandhi was a man from India who led opposition to British presence in that country. He believed in truth. His philosophy is called Satyagraha. This means "truth-force," though it is often interpreted to stand for nonviolence. Gandhi's followers promoted civil disobedience as a way to stand up against unjust laws. Gandhi never promoted violence. Still, he was punished by being put in jail several times. Eventually, he led his people to freedom, though he was assassinated.

When you study history, consider whether dishonesty or honesty played a part in an historical event. Honesty is a trait that nations, as well as individuals, should have.

> **"**My life is my message.**"**
> —Mahatma Gandhi, Nationalist Leader

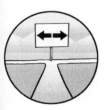

Being Honest in Life

Consider this situation:

Tyler was walking home from school when she spotted her friend Anna sitting on the porch of Liam's house. Tyler knew that Liam's parents were on vacation and that they had a strict policy against visitors when they were gone. On top of that, Anna and Liam were smoking, and Tyler knew Anna had told her parents she didn't smoke. Tyler waved to the pair and turned toward her own house. She had a great deal of homework to do that night and couldn't stop to talk.

When Tyler got home, she fixed a snack and settled onto the couch to start a reading assignment. The phone rang, and a moment later her mother came into the room and handed Tyler the phone. She told her it was Anna's mother. Taking the phone, Tyler was worried because she was sure that Anna's mother was going to ask her if she knew where Anna was. She took a deep breath and said, "Hello."

What would you tell Anna's mother? It may be okay not to say anything when being either honest or dishonest could cause you or others problems. For example, Tyler might tell Anna's mother that she knows Anna is safe. She could say she prefers that her mother ask Anna about her activities when she gets home. Combining honesty with caring for others is often a good combination.

Being Honest in Practice

For one day, be completely honest with one of your friends. This may mean not commenting on something that would be difficult to deal with instead of telling a "little white lie." You may tell the complete truth. Use your best judgment about the right thing to do to keep from hurting your friend.

You may be surprised by the consequences of being completely honest. Was it hard to do? Were you surprised by the responses you got? Did being honest cause you to hurt your friend's feelings in some way? Honesty without caring for other people is not necessarily a good thing.

HONESTY CHECKLIST

- ⬭ Don't lie.
- ⬭ Don't cheat.
- ⬭ Don't steal.
- ⬭ Don't say you'll do something that you don't intend to do.
- ⬭ Don't trick people.

> **"***Honesty is a good thing, but it is not profitable to its possessor unless it is kept under control.***"**
> —Don Marquis, Humorist

Honest Role Models

Here are people with a reputation for honesty. Though some of these people suffered for being honest, history remembers their achievements.

- Ralph Nader has championed the cause of honesty among American corporations. He has fought and won battles against car companies for improved safety standards and tobacco companies to get them to tell the truth about health risks from smoking.

- Henry David Thoreau lived in Colonial America. He went to jail for standing by his beliefs about free speech during the American Revolution. We remember him as an accomplished poet and advocate of the simple life.

- Oscar Wilde was a playwright and author of novels such as *The Portrait of Dorian Gray*. He lived in England during the Victorian period, a time with strict social codes. Through his writing and in his interactions, he challenged some hypocrisies of his age. Ironically, one of his best-known plays, *The Importance of Being Earnest*, centers on a series of lies, but Oscar himself suffered greatly for telling the truth.

> **❝**Aim above morality. Be not simply good; be good for something.**❞**
> —**Henry David Thoreau, Writer**

What's in It for Me?

Consider these real-life consequences of how you incorporate honesty in your character:

- People who are dishonest in the extreme may end up in serious trouble. They may even go to jail for crimes such as embezzlement (stealing money) or stealing.

- Honest people gain the trust and respect of others. They get and keep friends better than those who can't be trusted.

- Employers rank honesty as one of the most important traits in an employee. People who lie or steal on the job can be fired. This makes it difficult to find another job.

Related Words to Explore

Here are some words related to the trait of honesty and to its opposite, dishonesty:

- Dependable
- Responsible
- Sensitive
- Truthful
- Sincere

- Genuine
- Honorable
- Deceptive
- Evasive
- Unforthcoming

HUMBLE

Humble people are not focused on their achievements. They can be pleased with their successes, but their successes are not what interest them most. They are good at sharing praise with others. They recognize that everybody in a group contributes to an effort.

Do you consider yourself humble?

What Does It Mean to Be Humble?

Humble people are not overly proud or arrogant. They don't like to draw attention to themselves. Sometimes people seem humble because they're shy. Sometimes humble people are very self-confident. They don't need others to praise them to feel good about themselves.

The essence of being humble, whatever your reasons for it, is that you don't feel the need to be the center of attention. You realize that nobody is perfect and everyone has room for improvement.

Humble people often try to direct praise to others. For that reason, they are often seen as being generous. Have you met humble people?

> **"**Half of the harm that is done in this world is due to people who want to feel important.... They are absorbed in the endless struggle to think well of themselves.**"**
> —T. S. Eliot, Poet

Humbleness through Time

There have been many examples of humble characters in movies. Here are two:

- In the movie *Forrest Gump*, the main character had a low IQ. Throughout his life, he seemed to end up at the right place when an historic moment occurred, but he never seemed to appreciate what was happening. He was a kind person, a good friend and son, and a brave soldier. Still, he kept a humble attitude about himself and his achievements.

- *Mr. Holland's Opus* is about a music teacher who longs to be a composer. The need to support his family and help his deaf son forces him to keep working, never achieving his dream. However, at the end of the movie, he realizes that he achieved a great deal by teaching children to love music. He had been humble about his achievements because they were not what he had intended to do. However, his life was very worthwhile.

Sometimes people have great abilities in one area but wish to have abilities in another. When they are praised for their talent, they think it unimportant because it is not what they most want to be good at. They appear humble about something that others see as great. Are you good at something that you don't see as very special? Perhaps that's what you are most humble about.

Being Humble in Life

Consider this situation:

Chansawang had loved music all her life. She started studying flute when she was 5 years old. When she was 13, her music teacher entered her in a regional music contest. Chansawang practiced every day. When the day of the contest came, she won first prize. Going up on stage to receive her reward, she said this:

"Thank you. But this prize isn't really for me. It's for my father who taught me to really love music. He bought me a flute when I was just a little kid. It's for my music teacher, Mrs. Ready, who helps me sometimes by giving me extra sheet music to practice or extra help after school. It's also for all the kids in our school band who help each other learn to play new music all the time."

When Chansawang went home, she told her father she wanted to donate the $100 prize to the school fund for new band instruments.

If you were Chansawang's father, what would make you feel most proud, her musical talent or her humble character? Understanding that we are all special in certain ways and all flawed in others can be the basis of humility.

Being Humble in Practice

Are you involved in a group activity in which you excel? Are you the best swimmer on your team? Are you the one in the school play who sings the best? Next time your group has a success, look for ways to praise others, not thinking about getting praise yourself.

HUMBLENESS CHECKLIST

○ Don't focus on yourself, but on others.

○ Feel proud of your achievements, but share rewards with those who helped you.

○ Appreciate that everybody has strengths and weaknesses.

○ Take time to acknowledge other people's accomplishments.

○ Don't brag or boast.

Humble Role Models

Here are people known for being humble.

- Fred Astaire was possibly the greatest stage and movie dancer of all time. Still, this hard-working actor/singer/dancer avoided praise. He hated parties where people would recognize and flatter him. He was so uninterested in attention that, in his will, he said his life should never be the basis of a play or movie.

- C. S. Lewis was a teacher at Oxford University, a lecturer, and an author. He wrote fantasy and science fiction books such as *The Chronicles of Narnia* and *Out of the Silent Planet*. Lewis appeared publicly to lecture, but he did not like the limelight. Winston Churchill offered him a knighthood, but he turned it down.

- Emily Dickinson was a poet who lived a quiet life in Massachusetts from 1830–1886. For many years, she hardly ever left her house. She wrote 1,800 poems but had only 7 published while she was alive. Though her experiments with rhythm and metaphor had a great impact on modern poetry, she never made an effort to promote herself or her poems.

Can you recall a situation when you were humble? Why didn't you want rewards or attention for what you accomplished?

What's in It for Me?

Consider these real-life consequences of being humble:

- You don't need the recognition of others to feel good about your own achievements.

- You focus more on others' successes than on your own.

- You are seen by others as being generous and kind.

- You let others take center stage when rewards are being given, which makes you feel good.

Related Words to Explore

Here are some words related to the trait of being humble and to its opposite:

- Humility
- Retiring
- Modest
- Unassuming
- Unpretentious

- Self-effacing
- Meek
- Arrogant
- Inflated
- Boastful

> **"**Humility does not mean thinking less of yourself than of other people, nor does it mean having a low opinion of your own gifts. It means freedom from thinking about yourself at all.**"**
> —**William Temple, Statesman**

INNOVATIVE

Innovative people have a knack for coming up with new things. They might create a new way of doing something or develop a new approach to solving an old problem. They are not tied down to the way things have been done before. Instead, they break the mold and start anew.

Do you consider yourself an innovative person?

What Does It Mean to Be Innovative?

What's the difference between being creative and being innovative? These two traits are very closely related. A creative person brings something that never existed before into being, such as a painting or a piece of music. An innovative person also creates something new. Typically, creative people bring something artistic or beautiful alive, whereas an innovative person might develop a new process or approach to something.

An innovator might find a new process to mold silver, for example. A creative person might use that process to produce a piece of beautiful jewelry. Inventors are innovative; artists are creative. Is the distinction important? Not really. When you get down to it, innovative people and creative people share the ability to break from tradition. They find a new way to express themselves or a new way to make something happen.

Who do you know that you consider innovative?

Innovation through Time

There have been many examples of innovation in history, including these:

- The steam engine has been around in some fashion since the late 1700s. However, each engine was unique, and track sizes varied. James Watt patented an arrangement of wheels and cranks using a pattern card. He kept to certain kinds of parts and sizes, which created a standard. This standardization in engineering led to many advances in the industrial age. With standard parts, trains could run on a standard system of tracks all around the country. This standardization extended the reach of the railroad system and made public transportation possible.

- In the early days of the auto industry, Henry Ford came up with several innovations. He created the assembly line, which divided car assembly into several steps. Previously, one person might have done many tasks in manufacturing. In the assembly line, one person would work on one piece of the process, handing the car off to the next person in the line to do the next piece. Most manufacturing processes work the same way today. Ford also created the idea of the dealership to sell and service cars. He felt that business had to be local to succeed in selling to local people.

Innovators take a new approach to things that may revolutionize an industry or society. They don't just create a single piece of art; they create a new way of doing things in business, science, math, and other fields.

Being Innovative in Life

Consider this situation:

The students at Monroe Middle School had always put on the spring play in the auditorium. This year, however, they were told that the auditorium was being renovated in May to replace broken water pipes. The drama club sat down one afternoon to talk about the problem.

Alana suggested the students cancel the show. Marshall thought they should do the show in the high school auditorium. However, someone pointed out that the high school students were doing their musical during at that time. Caelyn sat listening to everybody's ideas and then raised her hand. "What if we use the school video camera and tape the play at the high school one evening when their play isn't running. Then we could put the video on the school Web site."

The students were quiet. They looked at the teacher, who was grinning. "That's a great idea," he said. "We'll do our own music video!" They started talking excitedly about how they could write their own play and music.

Sometimes innovation comes by bringing up an idea from the past and using it in a new way. Sometimes it comes from thinking of something completely new. Have you ever thought of a new way to accomplish something?

Being Innovative in Practice

Think of some process you do everyday: the route you take to get somewhere, a method for cooking food, or the way you organize your computer files. Now do it differently. Think through the steps first: Is there a better way to do things? Is there a more interesting way to achieve what you want to accomplish? Simply trying something in a new way makes you innovative and may help you discover a better way to get things done.

INNOVATION CHECKLIST

○ Look at things differently than others do.

○ Look for ways to do things better.

○ Explore different ideas without worrying too much about failure.

○ Don't be held back by the way things have always been done.

○ Take chances.

"There is a vitality, a life-force, an energy, a quickening that is translated through you into action and because there is only one of you in all of time, this expression is unique."
—Martha Graham, Choreographer

Innovative Role Models

Here are people active in various walks of life who are known for innovation.

- Le Corbusier, born Charles-Edouard Jeanneret, was a famous architect. Many consider him the most important architect of the twentieth century. He felt that architecture should be reinvented for an industrial age, so he created the International Style. He liked tall buildings, once proposing that the center of Paris be rebuilt with eighteen 60-story buildings. His innovative buildings often have unusual shapes and materials.

- Steven Spielberg is a movie director and producer who created a new style of Hollywood movie: the blockbuster. His movies use older movie styles and blend them with impressive special effects. Movies such as *Raiders of the Lost Ark, E.T. the Extra-Terrestrial, Jurassic Park,* and *Close Encounters of the Third Kind* explore a mix of science fiction and fantasy in bold new ways.

People who innovate aren't held back by what's been done before. In fact, they often take what's been done and reinvent it in exciting new ways. Is there something you've done the same way for a long time you could do differently? You may find that something new works better.

> **"**The problem is never how to get new, innovative thoughts into your mind, but how to get old ones out. Every mind is a building filled with archaic furniture. Clean out a corner of your mind and creativity will instantly fill it.**"**
>
> —**Dee Hock, Founder of VISA International**

What's in It for Me?

Consider these real-life consequences of being innovative:

- You are constantly exploring new experiences.

- You can inspire others to open their minds to new ideas.

- You can be at the forefront of exciting new efforts.

- People see you as a creative and groundbreaking person.

- Innovative people often find great success when they happen on a new idea that becomes popular.

Related Words to Explore

Here are some words related to the trait of being innovative and to its opposite:

- Ground-breaking
- Pioneering
- Inventive
- Original
- Modern

- Forward-looking
- Traditional
- Redundant
- Common

INQUISITIVE

Inquisitive people are curious. They want to know more about things. They aren't afraid to ask questions. They usually don't worry about admitting what they don't know. They like to explore, learn, and discover things.

Are you an inquisitive person?

What Does It Mean to Be Inquisitive?

Being inquisitive means that you like to learn or are naturally curious about what makes things or people tick. Instead of accepting other's ideas, inquisitive people gather facts from several sources and then form their own opinions.

Of course, there is such a thing as being too inquisitive, in which case people see you as nosy or meddling. Inquisitive people would do well to respect the privacy of others and know when it's appropriate to ask questions and when it's not.

Inquisitive people may ask questions for different reasons. A scholar may be inquisitive to learn. A spy may be inquisitive to uncover a secret. Engineers are inquisitive about how machines work. Why do you ask questions?

Inquisitiveness through Time

Inquisitive episodes in history are intriguing, though not always positive:

- The Spanish Inquisition came about because Christian people in Spain resented successful Jewish people. Some of these Jews had supposedly converted to Christianity. Actually, they pretended to convert to avoid persecution. The Inquisition was begun to cleanse the society from heretics and to bring Spain one religion. The Inquisition involved seizing personal property, trials, and the questioning and torture of suspects to uncover heresy.

- The Age of Enlightenment is a term used for the eighteenth century. At that time, intellectuals stressed reason, progress, and discovery. They questioned old ways of doing things and traditional authority. During this age, literacy spread to the public. Isaac Newton lived during this time, as did Descartes, a philosopher who supported rationalism. Rationalism is a philosophy that values observation and experience over learned knowledge. The trend of inquisitiveness in this century saw advances in science, math, philosophy, and social principles.

Inquiry has been used as a tool of persecution as well as learning. People have been put on trial to question their beliefs. Scientists have studied to further our knowledge. A person's motivations for being inquisitive may say a lot about him or her.

Being Inquisitive in Life

Consider this situation:

Tania had to write a report on a colorful character from the American West. She chose Calamity Jane, a sharpshooter who was featured in Wild West shows. Tania got information on Jane from the encyclopedia and from visiting several Web sites.

What Tania learned made her curious. So, after handing in her report, she wrote a letter to a museum. The museum had materials about Calamity Jane's life. They sent her a packet full of information, including photos. Tania decided to write an article about Jane, which she submitted to a kid's magazine. When she received a letter from the magazine telling her the article would be published, she couldn't believe it. The letter included a check for $100. Tania used some of the money to buy books about women of the West to learn more.

Inquisitive people love knowledge for its own sake. Learning one thing often sparks an interest in learning more. These people may use their knowledge in different ways, sharing it with others by writing or becoming a teacher or researcher. Are you inquisitive about a particular topic?

> **"**What we have to do is be forever curiously testing new opinions and courting new impressions.**"**
> —**Walter Pater, Essayist**

Being Inquisitive in Practice

Pick a topic that interests you and spend a day learning about it. Ask people what they know about it. Research the topic online. Read articles or a book about the topic. At the end of the day, you will know a lot more than you did before.

Did your research bring up other questions or topics of interest? Can you ever know everything there is to know about something? Can you ever be too inquisitive?

INQUISITIVENESS CHECKLIST

- ◯ Don't take things at face value.
- ◯ Ask questions if you don't understand something instead of pretending that you do.
- ◯ Use various resources to learn, such as the Internet, books, and television.
- ◯ Look into the background of things, people, and events.
- ◯ Use opportunities to talk to many people to learn what they know.

❝The cure for boredom is curiosity. There is no cure for curiosity.**❞**
—Dorothy Parker, Writer

Inquisitive Role Models

Here are some people in various walks of life. Each has a reputation for being inquisitive:

- Isaac Newton was the son of a farmer. He took courses in philosophy, law, and mathematics. He made discoveries in mathematics, optics (light), physics, and astronomy and was the creator of calculus. He invented the reflecting telescope and wrote about light being composed of a spectrum of colors. He is perhaps best known for his theory of gravity.

- Dian Fossey was an anthropologist who went to live in a remote area of Rwanda in Africa. She studied the habits of a certain type of mountain gorilla. Because hunters often killed or captured the animals, they were in danger of extinction. Fossey lived among the gorillas for 18 years to study their behavior. She dedicated her life to learning about and protecting them.

- H.L. Mencken was a newspaper reporter who lived from 1880 to 1956. He wrote reviews, articles, and commentaries on a wide variety of topics. It is part of a reporter's job to discover the facts of a situation and tell that information to others. It's a safe bet that most reporters, including Mencken, are inquisitive by nature.

Most people are inquisitive about things that interest them. Some people, like Isaac Newton, have a wide range of interests and enjoy learning about most things. What do you like to learn about?

What's in It for Me?

Consider these real-life consequences of being inquisitive:

- You are constantly learning new things.

- You get information you need to get things done or do your job.

- You may become a successful reporter or scientist or get some other job that requires an inquisitive nature.

- You may make new discoveries.

- People consider you to be well informed.

Related Words to Explore

Here are some words related to the trait of being inquisitive and to its opposite:

- Questioning
- Curious
- Probing
- Interested
- Prying

- Nosy
- Apathetic
- Unquestioning
- Unimaginative

> **❝**Nothing in life is to be feared. It is only to be understood.**❞**
> —Marie Curie, Scientist

JOYFUL

To be joyful means that you are capable of being delighted by people and situations. Joyful people are made happy by beautiful things or when good things happen to others. What makes a person joyful may vary, but joyful people take time to notice the good things in life and celebrate them.

What Does It Mean to Be Joyful?

Everybody has difficult times in his or her life. Some people are rich and others poor. Some have physical challenges. Sometimes somebody who is poor or has challenges still takes joy in the world and other people.

To some degree, joyfulness is a personality trait. Some people are naturally more happy. But anybody has the capacity for joy. By working on your attitude and taking time to appreciate things that please you, you can become more joyful.

What makes you happy? Does a beautiful sunset bring you joy? Does a certain song or type of music make you feel happy? Will a warm, sunny, summer day bring a smile to your face? Focus on the things that bring joy, and you may just become joyful!

Joyfulness through Time

There have been many examples of joyfulness in the arts, including these:

- Charles Schultz, creator of the Peanuts cartoon, once said, "I don't think I'm a true artist....But I can draw pretty well and I can write pretty well, and I think I'm doing the best with whatever abilities I have been given. And what more can one ask?" This willingness to be happy with what one has is typical of joyful people. Schultz's comic strip looked at the world through children's eyes. The humor in Schultz's young cartoon characters is still enjoyed today.

- A Marc Chagall painting titled "Joy" presents a variety of images. At the center of the picture are a man and woman floating above a river, hugging each other. Next to them is a tree with a face peering out of it. Above them are a man reading a book and an animal tooting a horn floating through the sky. At their feet lies another man playing a violin. The picture brings nature, music, and love together in a joyful moment.

People use art to show what makes them both happy and sad. Cartoons are typically humorous and make us smile. Paintings can reflect the beauty of nature that brings us joy. What art makes you joyful? Have you ever studied a picture or listened to a song and just felt good?

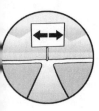

Being Joyful in Life

Consider this situation:

> Josh's family had rented a vacation house on the beach. On their last night at the beach, they were going to drive into a nearby town. They planned to go to the premiere of a new sci-fi movie. Josh, his brothers, and his parents were looking forward to a fun last night of vacation.
>
> When Josh's father tried to start the car, it wouldn't start. Something was wrong with it. His father came back in the house and told the family their big night was off. Josh's brothers were disappointed and started to quarrel. His parents sat at the dining table worrying about how much it would cost to fix the car.
>
> Josh went to the kitchen and packed the picnic hamper. Then he said, "Hey, we have one more night at the beach. Let's not spend it fighting. I packed some stuff for a cookout. Let's have fun with the time we have left!" With that, he strode outside, grabbing the radio and turning it on to some music.

Joyful people have a capacity to find the good in situations. They would rather be happy than sad, so they act happy. Is that all it takes to be happy—to decide to be? Sometimes it is!

Being Joyful in Practice

Look for an event today that you can feel joyful about. Perhaps a friend wins a sports event. Instead of envying her, can you feel joy for her? Is there a beautiful piece of music that you can really stop and enjoy? Take time to find joy in something or someone.

That wasn't so hard, was it?

JOYFULNESS CHECKLIST

○ Expose yourself to the things in life that make you happy.

○ Take the time to slow down and allow yourself to feel joy every day.

○ Look on the positive side of things.

○ Feel joy in your own and others' accomplishments.

○ Appreciate beautiful things.

"We are cups, constantly and quietly being filled. The trick is knowing how to tip ourselves over and let the Beautiful Stuff out.**"**

—Ray Bradbury, Writer

Joyful Role Models

Here are some people in various walks of life. Although it's difficult to know what a life is really like unless you've lived it, each of these people appears to have known how to feel joy.

- Bob Hope was a comedian and one of the most successful performers of his century. In the entertainment industry, you seldom see someone with such a stable personal and professional life. Hope received five honorary Academy Awards and entertained troops in every war since World War II, until his death. Hope once said, "I have seen what a laugh can do. It can transform almost unbearable tears into something bearable, even hopeful."

- Dr. Joyce Brothers is a psychologist who has been in the public eye as a writer and TV personality. She stresses finding healthy balances between work and emotions. She encourages people to be happy in their lives.

- Deepak Chopra is an author and physician. He has written books about a balance of body, mind, and spirit. A positive spirit can have a strong effect on the body. Chopra brought together ideas from ancient cultures with concepts from science. His search for the healthy person is a combination of spirit, mind, and the physical body, all working in joyful purpose.

Joyful people can be found in every walk of life. Typically, they enjoy what they do. Many of them help others find happiness through their work.

What's in It for Me?

Consider these real-life consequences of being joyful:

- You enjoy life and appreciate all it has to offer.

- You celebrate your own successes and those of others.

- You are seen as a positive and fun person to be around.

- You are often the person to show others a more positive way to resolve a conflict.

Related Words to Explore

Here are some words related to the trait of being joyful and to its opposite:

- Exuberant
- Optimistic
- Happy
- Positive
- Lively
- Cheerful

- Excited
- Lethargic
- Sad
- Reserved
- Pessimistic

> **"**The talent for being happy is appreciating and liking what you have, instead of what you don't have.**"**
> —Woody Allen, Writer, Actor, and Director

LEADER

Leaders are not people who know everything. They may have to count on others to provide technical or political or business expertise. But leaders can grab ahold of a vision and inspire others to reach it. Leaders can also make difficult decisions without hesitation.

Have you ever acted like a leader?

What Does It Mean to Be a Leader?

Leadership is a very complex trait. Some people have been great leaders but have had too much personal ambition or greed. Leadership itself is the ability to get people excited about a goal and guide them to reach it. Leaders often depend on many other people to reach a goal. But they have a knack of inspiring and rewarding people.

When tough choices have to be made, a true leader will first weigh all the information and advice. Then he or she will make a choice without hesitating. This ability gives those following that person confidence in both the leader and the leader's goal.

With leadership comes great responsibility. A leader should respect those following him or her and recognize that little is accomplished by a single person. A good leader should listen to advice and reward those who work hard. Finally, a good leader should never let the power that a leader is often given go to his or her head.

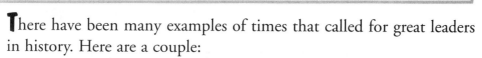 

Leadership through Time

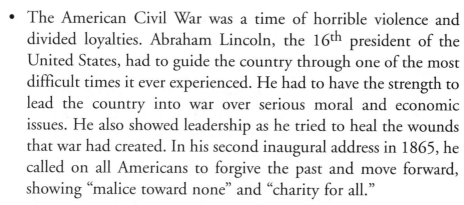

There have been many examples of times that called for great leaders in history. Here are a couple:

- The American Civil War was a time of horrible violence and divided loyalties. Abraham Lincoln, the 16th president of the United States, had to guide the country through one of the most difficult times it ever experienced. He had to have the strength to lead the country into war over serious moral and economic issues. He also showed leadership as he tried to heal the wounds that war had created. In his second inaugural address in 1865, he called on all Americans to forgive the past and move forward, showing "malice toward none" and "charity for all."

- When King Henry VIII died, he left England in turmoil. His only son died shortly after he did, and his two daughters, Elizabeth and Mary, followed different religions. This religious division was affecting their country. As the younger daughter, Elizabeth I of England had not expected to become queen. Still she cooperated with people who wanted to overthrow her sister. One of her strengths as a leader came from her ability to choose capable people and listen to their advice. When she took the throne, her country was poor and split apart with religious differences. When she died 45 years later, England was one of the most prosperous and powerful countries in the world.

The world has known many difficult times. Those who have stepped forward to lead in those times have had great challenges. A great leader is often one who understands his or her own limitations. This type of leader seeks advice and support from others. What a leader can provide is a spark of inspiration, insight, or moral courage that a group or country needs.

Being a Leader in Life

Consider this situation:

> *Jessie loved music, and he played trumpet in the school band. He wasn't the best player, but he was very enthusiastic. Before class, he would talk to other kids and get them excited about tackling a new piece of music or the upcoming concert.*
>
> *When Mr. Harvey, the music teacher, was out sick, he would tell the substitute teacher that Jessie could conduct in his place. Jessie had a way of getting the other kids to focus and play their music. But he also would make the classes fun.*
>
> *A week before the concert, Mr. Harvey asked Jessie to stay after class. "Jessie," he said, "how would you like to conduct the concert? These kids really respect you and listen to you, and I'd like to see you have the chance to lead them." Jessie was thrilled, and rushed home to tell his father.*

Some people have a natural talent for leadership. Others listen to them, and they can get others to be enthusiastic. Even if you aren't a natural leader, you can develop leadership qualities. You can learn how to communicate your excitement and vision and treat people with respect so they respect you.

> **"** The final test of a leader is that he leaves behind him in other men the conviction and will to carry on. **"**
>
> —**Walter Lippmann, American Journalist**

Being a Leader in Practice

Do you feel you can contribute a vision and direction in some situation? Step forward and take the lead. Find ways to motivate others, and don't forget to reward them. Keep others excited about the goal, and give them what they need to do their part.

LEADERSHIP CHECKLIST

○ Find a worthwhile goal, and lead others to it.

○ Treat those who follow you with kindness, respect, and loyalty.

○ Appreciate that everybody has strengths and weaknesses.

○ Take time to acknowledge other people's contributions.

○ Understand your own weaknesses, and gather people around you who can make up for them.

> **"***Leaders are visionaries with a poorly developed sense of fear and no concept of the odds against them. They make the impossible happen.***"**
> —Dr. Robert Jarvik, Heart Surgeon

Leadership Role Models

Here are some people from various walks of life. Each of these people is known for being a good leader.

- During World War II, Dwight D. Eisenhower was appointed as the Supreme Commander of the Allied forces in December 1943. He commanded the forces of the invasion of Normandy. As a soldier, he showed great leadership, helping to increase cooperation among the Allied forces. Eisenhower's ability to make the many hard decisions involved in war, coupled with his diplomatic abilities, made him an effective leader.

- Napoleon Bonaparte, Emperor of France, was a brilliant strategist in war and a great administrator. He was also an ambitious dictator. Napoleon's early leadership style included promising rewards to his badly treated soldiers and going into battle with them, showing great courage. His intelligence and bravery won over his troops.

People who are good leaders have a flair and style that convince others to follow them. Their motives and goals may differ. Napoleon was personally ambitious, Eisenhower served a cause, but both showed the spark of great leaders. If you were a leader, would you lead people for selfish gain or to help the world?

> **"** Being powerful is like being a lady. If you have to tell people you are, you aren't. **"**
> —Margaret Thatcher, Former Prime Minister of England

What's in It for Me?

Consider these real-life consequences of being a leader:

- You have the opportunity to inspire others to action.

- You can create a sense of purpose in yourself and others.

- You have skills in managing people or making tough decisions that will help you move forward in your career.

- You can feel good about your accomplishments.

Related Words to Explore

Here are some words related to the trait of being a leader and to its opposite:

- Guide
- Manager
- Visionary
- Chief

- Boss
- Director
- Underling
- Follower

> **"**I never did anything alone. Whatever was accomplished**"**
> in this country was accomplished collectively.
> —**Golda Meir, Prime Minister of Israel**

LOYAL

Being loyal consists of being faithful to something or somebody, even when doing so is difficult. Loyalty involves a basic belief in the rightness of something that you stick with through thick and thin. People can be loyal to their country, their family, their sports team, or their employer, for example.

What are you loyal to?

What Does It Mean to Be Loyal?

Because there is so much change in our lives, it is often challenging to be loyal. A person is loyal to his team, until it starts losing games. Someone is loyal to a friend, until he hits hard times. An individual is loyal to her country, until the government does something she disagrees with.

Loyal people stick with something even when times are rough or disagreements occur. They are committed to the basic idea of the cause or person they are loyal to, even if there are occasional disagreements or difficulties.

Of course, the basic idea of a cause or person sometimes changes, and our loyalties may change as a result. However, being thoughtful about when and why to make those changes is at the heart of being loyal.

Loyalty through Time

Here are examples from history and from literature that required loyalty:

- Paul Revere was an American patriot who took part in the Boston Tea Party and made the famous midnight ride to Lexington, Massachusetts, warning people of the approach of British troops. Though his role in the American Revolution has been romanticized in poems and stories, he was no doubt a loyal patriot who risked his life to protest and protect against the British.

- Gunga Din was the subject of a poem by Rudyard Kipling. According to the poem, during the British occupation of India, a local man named Gunga Din worked as a water carrier for the British troops. He was always loyal to them. The poem tells of Din giving water to wounded soldiers during battle. During one of these rescues, Din was killed. The poem praises the man's unquestioning loyalty. Even though his position in the group was humble, the poem ends by saying he was a better man than the rest because of his extreme loyalty.

> **"**The secret to a good life is to have the right loyalties and hold them in the right scale of values.**"**
> —Norman Thomas, Socialist and Politician

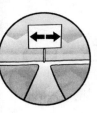

Being Loyal in Life

Consider this situation:

Theresa had worked a couple of summers for a local video store called Movies and More. Over the winter, a new chain store had moved into town. The chain had built a big store with three times as many titles as Movies and More. The day before Theresa was supposed to start her summer job at Movies and More, the manager of the new store called her.

The new store's manager had heard Theresa was an experienced clerk. He wondered whether she would be interested in a job at his store. He told her he could pay $2.50 more an hour than Movies and More. Plus, she could get a discount on video and DVD rentals. Theresa told him she would think about his offer.

Theresa went to her dad to talk over the situation. Her dad pointed out that the owner of Movies and More had given Theresa her first job and had treated her well. "Over the summer, you might earn a few hundred dollars more, but you don't know how this new manager is to work for," her father noted. "It's up to you," he said, "but don't let the money alone make up your mind. There are more important things in life."

The next morning Theresa reported to work at Movies and More, noting the relief in her boss's eyes. At the end of the summer, Theresa received a surprise bonus.

Sometimes loyalty may cause you to lose extra money or glory. But the value of loyalty is that you feel part of something. You don't desert people when they are down, and you often are rewarded when things get better. Have you ever had to choose between loyalty and money? What decision did you make?

Being Loyal in Practice

Is there a cause, group, or person to whom you could show loyalty? Consider how committed you are to this person or thing. Do you attend every meeting? Are you ready to help when asked? Do you truly feel a part of something bigger than yourself? Try showing loyalty, and see how it feels and what rewards you find.

LOYALTY CHECKLIST

- Be thoughtful in choosing the things and people you ally yourself with.

- Stick with your commitments even in difficult times.

- Keep the vision that first attracted you to a cause, organization, or person.

- Don't allow money or other offers of reward alone to change your loyalties.

- Check in occasionally to make sure the things that first caused you to commit are still in place.

Loyal Role Models

Here are people who are known for being loyal.

- Larry Bird was a basketball player superstar. He started with an ailing Boston Celtics team in 1979 and stayed with it his entire 13-year career. He helped turn the team around and bring it to the top of its division. He was known for inspiring teammates to excel, working for the glory of the team. Though he spent his last few seasons in and out of surgery for back problems, he made an impressive showing whenever he played in a game. Finally, he retired in 1997 to coach. Considering he could have used his superstar status to join any team he liked, his 13-year run of loyalty to one team is impressive.

- Hillary Clinton is the wife of Bill Clinton, 42nd President of the United States. She is now a senator from New York. During her husband's time in office, she worked for various human rights issues. When Congress impeached her husband, she stood by him loyally. Since he left office, she has pursued her own career, becoming a senator. In fact, no First Lady of the United States has ever sought political office before. Through it all, however, Senator Clinton remains loyal to her husband.

You may be loyal to a team, a country, or a person. That loyalty may be difficult to give as the person or group you have attached yourself to goes through difficult times. The first step in loyalty is to think through carefully the allegiance you are making. If it is the right allegiance, it may be worth keeping through time. Have you been loyal to a person or organization even in difficult times?

What's in It for Me?

Loyal people can reap many benefits. For example, they can

- Earn loyalty from others.

- Reap financial or other benefits when the thing or person they are loyal to succeeds.

- Be seen as a desirable employee by employers.

- Feel the excitement of being part of a winning team if they have been loyal through good and bad times.

Related Words to Explore

Here are some words related to the trait of being loyal and to its opposite:

- Faithful
- Devoted
- Steadfast
- Dedicated
- Constant

- Reliable
- Disloyal
- Traitorous
- Treacherous
- Unfaithful

OPEN-MINDED

People who are open-minded don't prejudge. They are willing to listen to new ideas and different opinions. Open-minded people tend not to judge others based on their race or gender or beliefs. They wait to see what a person is like before drawing conclusions.

In what ways are you open-minded?

What Does It Mean to Be Open-Minded?

Some people learn one way of looking at things and never change their minds. Others explore different ideas and ways of looking at things. Sometimes these open-minded people change their minds and look at things differently. They may be open to accepting differences among people as well as new ideas.

As children, we are taught many things. Some things are right, and some things are right at the time, or right for the people who teach them to us. The ability to stay open and listen to other ideas allows us to learn and make our own choices.

When somebody expresses an idea that is different from what you believe, do you automatically shut that person out? What would happen if you listened to that person and used your intelligence to come to your own conclusions?

Open-Mindedness through Time

Examples of open-minded societies exist in the history of religion:

- Roger Williams was the founder of the Rhode Island colony. He created the earliest principles of religious freedom in what was then the new American colony. Like many immigrants, he had moved to America to escape persecution for his religious beliefs. Unfortunately, some of the new colonies practiced their own form of religious intolerance. The Rhode Island colony welcomed Jewish people and Quakers and other groups of Christians. Their open-mindedness created the early idea of separation of church and state, in which religion does not control the laws and actions of the government.

- Often because early religious documents stated that only men could be ordained, religions have excluded women from being ministers or priests. In America, the Quaker religion was the first to allow women ministers in the early 1800s. The Congregationalist Church ordained a woman minister in 1853, followed by the Universalist Church in 1863. Though men have traditionally been priests and ministers, many religions have opened the role to women.

Society changes over time. Change brings new ideas and new attitudes. Some open-minded people may accept change. Open-minded people don't always buy into a new way of doing things. However, they are at least willing to hear about them and make up their minds instead of prejudging them.

Being Open-Minded in Life

Consider this situation:

> The boys in Jake's neighborhood had started to organize a baseball team. Over the summer, they planned to play against a team from the nearby neighborhood in the park. Though they had a few guys, they needed a couple more. They put up signs around the park saying they were holding tryouts on Saturday.
>
> On Saturday, a new kid in town, Joshua, showed up, along with Charlie from two streets over. Just as they were about to start the tryouts, Jessica walked up. "I want to try out for the team," she announced.
>
> The guys laughed at the idea of a girl on their team but soon realized Jessica was serious. One guy said to let her try out because she'd never make the team. First, Joshua hit and pitched a few balls, and he was pretty good. Then Charlie got up to bat. Charlie couldn't hit a single ball, and his pitching was worse. Then Jessica was up. She hit every ball and struck out the team's best player when she pitched.

Who do you think the guys picked for their team? Would they be open-minded about having a girl on the team? Women have become more accepted in certain sports these days, but it took people being open-minded to bring those changes. Who would you pick for the team?

> **❝**Where there is an open mind, there will always be a frontier. **❞**
> —**Charles Kettering, Inventor**

Being Open-Minded in Practice

If you are completely against something, take the time to learn more about both sides of the issue. Talk to people who believe the opposite of what you believe. Try to keep an open mind as they tell you about their point of view. Did you learn something you didn't realize before? Did it change your mind?

OPEN-MINDEDNESS CHECKLIST

○ Don't prejudge people or issues.

○ Ask other people to explain their point of view to you.

○ Be willing to change your mind if the evidence suggests that your current ideas are wrong.

○ Allow for the fact that people have a right to believe different things.

○ Appreciate the differences among all people.

Open-Minded Role Models

Here are two people with a reputation for being open-minded.

- Bjorn Lomborg is a statistician from a university in Denmark. He studied evidence about our environment and drew conclusions that differ from most people. He feels that our planet is getting healthier. He has exposed some misleading use of evidence by environmental groups. Whether he is right or wrong, Lomborg has stayed open-minded in the face of current thinking about our environment and has focused on the facts.

- Javier Solana has been in charge of creating a foreign policy for the European Union, a group of 25 member countries. Solana has advised against knee-jerk anti-Americanism. In bringing so many countries with different cultures together, he has had to keep an open mind. For example, he spoke against NATO in the 1980s. By 1995, however, he had changed his mind and had become the Secretary-General of NATO. Clearly, Solana is willing to keep an open mind about international politics.

> **"**Feelings of worth can flourish only in an atmosphere where individual differences are appreciated, mistakes are tolerated, communication is open, and rules are flexible.**"**
> —**Virginia Satir, Therapist**

What's in It for Me?

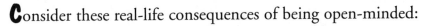

Consider these real-life consequences of being open-minded:

- You can see many sides to a question.

- People respect your ability to avoid prejudging people or situations.

- Because you don't prejudge things, you may learn and grow instead of shutting out new possibilities.

- You are open to the newest and best ideas that come along.

Related Words to Explore

Here are some words related to the trait of being open-minded and to its opposite:

- Unbiased
- Flexible
- Tolerant
- Unprejudiced

- Liberal
- Prejudiced
- Narrow-minded

PATIENT

Being patient means that you don't get upset if things take time to happen. You realize that you can't have everything you want now. Patience can help you stick with things when others have given up because you aren't in a rush to move on to the next thing.

Have you ever been patient with somebody or something?

What Does It Mean to Be Patient?

Some people feel rushed all the time, anxious when things don't happen right away. Others don't mind waiting for things to happen. They are patient people. Patient people know that they can't control everything and sometimes they just have to wait.

Patience can help you succeed. You may tackle larger projects because you have what it takes to see them through. You don't need immediate rewards but can look toward the future.

Do you know a patient person?

Patience through Time

Examples of patience exist in science and history:

- Those who observe nature have to be patient. For example, bird watchers and those who study the sky to observe planets need patience. John J. Audubon was a great bird fancier and painter. He painted incredibly detailed paintings of birds. For weeks or months, he would stay in the woods, waiting for the birds to appear. His studies helped to build a great catalog of the native birds of America. We still admire his artwork today.

- The Quaker religion stresses patient discussion and careful listening to each other. Quakers meet as a community to make decisions. One person might state a concern, and everybody else is expected to listen patiently. When somebody has something useful to say, he or she says it. This patient process of working things out involves the whole community.

Whether appreciating nature, which has its own rhythms, or appreciating the human spirit, patience plays a part. Taking the time to listen to the natural world or to other people requires that we not rush things. We must let them happen at their own speed. Patience isn't easy, but it can be rewarding.

> **"**It is very strange that the years teach us patience; that the shorter our time, the greater our capacity for waiting.**"**
> —Elizabeth Taylor, Actress

Being Patient in Life

Consider this situation:

> *Janet had been a math tutor for several years. When Ian started studying with her, he had trouble focusing. He always seemed eager to finish the lesson. When they reached a particularly hard lesson, at one point Ian threw up his hands and said, "I give up. This stuff is too hard." Janet agreed the topic was difficult, but she asked him to listen while she reviewed it one more time.*

> *The next week Janet reviewed the difficult lesson again. Ian said he understood a little bit more of what she was saying. Still, he had trouble with the problems. Every week Janet covered a little more of the lesson, and every week Ian understood it a little better. Finally, one day he understood the concept and answered all the problems correctly.*

Janet's patience with Ian paid off. Even though becoming frustrated would have been easy, she kept coming back to the topic until Ian mastered it. Patient people stick with things until they succeed. Do you think Ian learned a lesson beyond his math lesson from Janet? Would you have?

> **"**There is a way that nature speaks, that land speaks. Most of the time we are simply not patient enough, quiet enough, to pay attention to the story.**"**
>
> —**Chinese Proverb**

Being Patient in Practice

Is there something that you are always anxious to get done quickly? Try to take your time. If you rush through your homework, spend a little more time to get things right. If you play a game like chess but sometimes lose, take more time to consider the best strategy before you make your move. Did you find that patience paid off? Did you do something better than you do when you rush through it?

PATIENCE CHECKLIST

⭕ Don't rush things.

⭕ Take the time to do things right.

⭕ If something doesn't happen right away, wait for it to happen in its own time.

⭕ Take time to appreciate things in nature or other people.

⭕ Realize that not everybody or everything does things at the same pace as you. Appreciate the differences.

❝Our patience will achieve more than our force.❞

—Linda Hogan, Native American Poet and Novelist

Patient Role Models

Here are in people with a reputation for being patient.

- Admiral Hyman Rickover was born in Poland, then a part of Russia. His father was a tailor who brought his family to America. Rickover worked a full-time job through high school. Somebody recommended him for the U.S. Naval Academy. He graduated and then earned a master's degree. He entered the Navy but believed he could never make the rank of admiral because he was Jewish. There had never been a Jewish admiral. Rickover decided if he could work in a new area of the Navy where no social rules existed, he might be able to advance. He led a team developing the nuclear navy. He headquartered his group away from other Navy outposts so the social structure could begin fresh. By waiting and planning, Rickover built a successful career in a Navy that hadn't been ready for him when he started.

- Galileo Galilei was born in 1564 in Pisa, Italy. He studied medicine for four years because his father wanted him to, even though he hated it. He left school and tutored math, his great interest, for another four years. During those years, he spent time studying math, science, and philosophy. He then became a professor of math and astronomy. He taught courses about the sun and planets and the sun moving around the earth. Though his ideas often went against accepted thought, he patiently kept at work on them, eventually putting forth the theory that the earth moves around the sun.

What's in It for Me?

Consider these real-life consequences of being patient:

- People admire you for sticking with something until it is done.

- At work, others may consider you even-tempered and dependable.

- Your patience keeps you from getting too stressed or upset when things go wrong.

- Patience allows you to achieve things less patient people can't because they give up.

Related Words to Explore

Here are some words related to the trait of being patient and to its opposite:

- Enduring
- Tolerant
- Unhurried
- Persistent
- Uncomplaining

- Serene
- Impatient
- Edgy
- Urgent

> **"**Good ideas are not adopted automatically. They must be driven into practice with courageous patience.**"**
> —Titus Maccius Plautus, Roman Playwright

POLITE

Being polite means acting properly in social situations. Being polite also has a more old-fashioned meaning of being refined or cultivated. Polite people are considerate and speak and act with good manners. People often learn good manners when they are very small children.

Are you polite to people you meet?

What Does It Mean to Be Polite?

Manners are set in part by your culture's standards. European culture has different standards of politeness than Asian cultures, for example. What is polite in one country or at one time in history may not be polite in another place or time.

Certain things are expected of polite people in the United States. For example, you are expected to say "please" and "thank you," to hold a door open for the person behind you, not to interrupt people, and to write a thank-you note when you receive a gift. In another country, being polite may involve other words or actions.

No matter what the time or place, polite people are considerate of others and treat them with respect. When you are polite to people, usually they will be polite to you.

Young Person's Character Education Handbook, © JIST Life

Politeness through Time

Some characters in literature seem to embody politeness, for example:

- *Don Quixote*, written by Miguel de Cervantes, is about a deluded but idealistic man who sets out to single-handedly bring back an age of chivalry. He idealizes women and treats them with utmost courtesy. He champions the oppressed. Though on some levels this novel is a satire of traditional romances, the book presents a new form of chivalry. It is one with respect for others and the ability to see beyond the meanness of society to the best in people.

- In *Pygmalion*, written by George Bernard Shaw, a language teacher named Henry Higgins takes in a poor girl named Eliza Doolittle to teach her to speak better English. Higgins is himself rude to almost everybody. However, his friend, Colonel Pickering, is polite to everybody and helps Eliza learn manners. Though the play is in some ways a satire about polite manners and society, it shows the value of courtesy between people.

Often in literature or plays, characters are too polite. They have false manners and say things they don't mean. Being truly polite means you respect other people and believe everybody deserves to be treated well. Try not to let politeness become an insincere habit. Instead, show your respect for others by the things you say and do.

> **"**Politeness and consideration for others is like investing pennies and getting dollars back.**"**
> —Thomas Sowell, Author

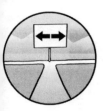

Being Polite in Life

Consider this situation:

Chloe's pen pal from England was visiting the United States with her mother. Chloe's mother invited them to their house for dinner. When Lydia and her mother arrived, they presented Chloe's parents with a china bowl from England as a gift and thanked them for the invitation. Chloe, her parents, and her brother Steven sat in the living room to talk. After a few minutes, the phone rang. Steven ran out of the room without saying a word. A minute later, he shouted, "Dad, it's for you!" Chloe's father shouted back, "Take a message, okay?"

Chloe noticed that Lydia and her mother looked uncomfortable. Maybe Steven should have excused himself before he left the room? She wondered whether Steven and her father shouting from room to room seemed rude to their guests. But her family did that all the time.

In a few minutes, they all went in to dinner. Chloe observed their guests. Lydia asked Chloe's mother to please pass the potatoes and thanked her when she did. At the end of the meal, Lydia's mother thanked Chloe's mother for a lovely dinner. Chloe's family got up from the table without thanking her mother for the dinner.

In your family, you may have put aside polite behavior because you are so familiar with each other. Do you say "please" and "thank you" to each other? Do you excuse yourself if you leave the dinner table? Do you shout to someone in the next room? When we meet people from different cultures, we sometimes see ourselves through their eyes and their standards of politeness. What do you think Lydia and her mother thought of Chloe's family? What would they think of yours?

Being Polite in Practice

Is there somebody you have not been very polite to in the past? Perhaps you don't say "please" and "thank you" to your brother. Or maybe you haven't taken the time to thank a friend or teacher for helping you. Try being polite to everybody you meet today. Hold the door for someone in a store. Say "please" when asking for something. Study the reactions you get when you treat people with politeness. Do they seem friendlier to you?

POLITENESS CHECKLIST

○ Always remember to say "please" and "thank you."

○ Say "excuse me" if you interrupt somebody or walk in front of others in a public place.

○ Treat people as you would like to be treated.

○ Ask permission to do things in other people's homes instead of assuming you can take or do what you wish.

○ Bring a gift when you are invited to somebody's home, and send a thank-you note after.

Polite Role Models

Here are some people who have a reputation for being polite:

- Japanese people are known for being polite. They have many rules of etiquette that keep their large society in order. Bowing is the Japanese version of a handshake. They are extremely punctual and clean. At the entry to homes or buildings, people take off their shoes and put on slippers. In Japan, it is impolite to eat or drink while walking down the street, blow your nose in public, or shout at someone to get his or her attention.

- Queen Elizabeth II, the Queen of England since 1953, was brought up to be polite and courteous. It is her job to represent the British monarchy and the British people to others. She is bound by traditions of politeness and social courtesies that are hundreds of years old. Though, like all of us, she may have less polite moments in private, in public she seems calm and gracious to everyone, whether that person is a king or a laborer.

In the past, rich people and noble people like queens and kings were seen as more polite than other people. They developed elaborate traditions for politeness and looked down on those who did not know those traditions. This was one way of keeping divisions between people in society. Today, we all have the opportunity to be polite and to learn polite behavior. Study people you consider polite to learn how to be more polite yourself.

> **"**Life is not so short but that there is always time enough for courtesy.**"**
> —Ralph Waldo Emerson, Essayist and Poet

What's in It for Me?

Consider these real-life consequences of being polite:

- People find you pleasant to be with.

- You make and keep friends.

- You avoid conflict with others.

- You are welcome as a guest.

- People are more polite to you.

- You think of others' feelings and are therefore somebody who does well dealing with people from different cultures.

Related Words to Explore

Here are some words related to the trait of being polite and to its opposite:

- Civil
- Gracious
- Well-mannered
- Courteous
- Respectful

- Refined
- Rude
- Obnoxious
- Ill-mannered

POSITIVE

Being positive means you always believe things will work out. You focus on the good in things, not the bad. Positive people don't worry about what could go wrong. Instead, they find ways to make things go right.

Can you think of a time when being positive helped you achieve something you didn't think was possible?

What Does It Mean to Be Positive?

Sometimes focusing on success can make it happen. When people feel they cannot fail, they often succeed.

If you don't think you can do something, the odds are that you can't because your attitude defeats you. If you believe you can do something, if you feel positive, then you might. Are positive people always successful? No. They have failures. But they don't let fear of failure stop them from trying. They don't let failure get them down in the long term.

After all, if you don't try something, you'll never succeed. If you do, sometimes you will reach your goal.

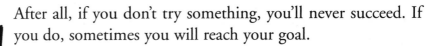

"*The positive thinker sees the invisible, feels the intangible, and achieves the impossible.***"**
—Anonymous

Positiveness through Time

There have been many examples of being positive in history. Here are a couple:

- Getting information and mail across the United States back in the mid-1800s as the population spread west was a challenge. There were no railroads, buses, road systems, or cars. Three men founded the Pony Express, which used riders to carry mail and news by horse across this huge country. It took about 75 horses to make a trip from Missouri to California, with riders changing horses at relay stations. The riders had to deal with rough terrain, bad weather, and hostile conditions. However, the three men who started the Pony Express were positive about their goal to set up a system of riders and relay stations. In doing so, they kept the country in contact during the difficult years of the Civil War.

- The field of aviation has known many people with positive attitudes. They include the Wright Brothers, who made the first recorded U.S. flight at Kitty Hawk, North Carolina, and Burt Rutan, who was the first person to fly solo around the world without refueling. Since the Wright Brothers, aviators have been driven to do the impossible. Through a combination of engineering, scientific know-how, and courage, these positive people take on difficult challenges every day.

People who try very difficult, if not impossible, things must have a positive attitude. They have to think about success, not failure. They look on the bright side. In what way are you a positive person? Could you be more positive in certain areas of your life? What would the result be?

Being Positive in Life

Consider this situation:

When he was 12, Marcus was diagnosed with a rare disease. Every week he had to undergo treatments in a hospital. He spent weeks unable to go to school. Most of the time, he felt weak and tired.

Instead of giving up, Marcus decided to be as positive as possible. He was pleasant and polite to all the nurses and technicians he met. He asked his stepmother if he could get a tutor to help him keep up with schoolwork. When he couldn't go to school, he did some research on the computer about his disease. He started a Web page where people with the disease could talk to each other about it.

After a year of treatments, Marcus was better. Even after he went back to school full time, he kept up his Web site to help others.

People who have to go through difficult times can give in to their problems. Or they can keep a positive attitude, which helps them get through. Positive people usually take action instead of sitting still.

When you have a problem, do you tackle it? Or do you let it get to you?

> **"**Few things in the world are more powerful than a positive push. A smile. A word of optimism and hope. A 'you can do it' when things are tough.**"**
>
> —**Richard M. DeVos, Founder of Amway Corporation**

Being Positive in Practice

Pick some challenge you haven't tackled because you were worried about failing. Take on that challenge. Decide that the possible reward outweighs any worry about failure. Don't let anything or anyone stop you from reaching your goal.

POSITIVENESS CHECKLIST

- ◯ Don't let yourself become discouraged.
- ◯ Always focus on the best possible outcome.
- ◯ Realize that even if you fail, you achieve something important by trying.
- ◯ Don't let negative people get you down.
- ◯ Understand that problems are just opportunities to learn.

> **"**A strong positive mental attitude will create more miracles than any wonder drug.**"**
> —Patricia Neal, Actress

Positive Role Models

Here are some everyday people like you and me. Each of these people has taken a positive action.

- Shauna Fleming was a 16-year-old high school student in 2004 when her father urged her to tackle a community project. She launched a campaign she called "A Million Thanks." The campaign asked people to write letters to the U.S. troops in Iraq. The millionth letter arrived only seven months after Shauna started the campaign. She then revised her goal to 1.4 million letters, which she reached in 2005. She is now working on founding branches of A Million Thanks at other high schools. Her positive attitude made this huge task possible.

- After John Davidson found out his son had a form of a disease called muscular dystrophy, he and his wife began working to help find a cure. In the summer of 1995, John pushed his son across Ontario, Canada, in a wheelchair. In all, they covered 3,300 kilometers. The trip raised funds for research to find a cure. They raised $1.5 million from people who donated to the cause. But that wasn't enough. In 1998, John walked across all of Canada (more than 8,300 kilometers), this time without his son. He raised $2 million in donations to create an endowment fund named after his son to continue the research.

People don't have to be famous to do something great. A positive spirit and belief in yourself can lead you to do amazing things. Being positive sometimes means going after a goal even if it seems impossible.

What could you achieve if you didn't believe you could fail?

What's in It for Me?

Consider these real-life consequences of being positive:

- You learn from failures and use what you learn to succeed the next time.

- You don't let things get you down but always look on the bright side.

- You achieve things others can't because they get discouraged from the start.

- You inspire others to try the impossible.

- At work, people find your positive attitude inspiring.

Related Words to Explore

Here are some words related to the trait of being positive and to its opposite:

- Upbeat
- Optimistic
- Constructive
- Affirmative
- Self-confident

- Negative
- Pessimistic
- Downbeat
- Discouraging
- Critical

RESOURCEFUL

Resourceful people are able to come up with what's needed to complete a task in almost any situation. They come up with a way to stretch food one more day when they're snowed in. They figure out how to fix the copier machine with only tape and a paperclip. They use what they have at hand to get the job done.

Can you remember a situation in which you were resourceful?

What Does It Mean to Be Resourceful?

When you are faced with a problem and the usual solutions won't help, what do you do? Resourceful people look around, use whatever is at hand, and come up with a fix. In difficult times such as during war or a natural disaster, resourceful people can be very handy to have around. They think of ways to get through a difficult time when other people have given up.

Resourcefulness is really made up of several traits: part courage, part cleverness, part creativity, and part innovation. Resourceful people don't give up as easily as others because problems are an interesting challenge to them.

Does somebody in your life always seem to come up with a solution to problems or figure out how to get things done? That's a resourceful person.

Resourcefulness through Time

You'll find many resourceful people in literature, for example:

- In the novel *Robinson Crusoe* by Daniel Defoe, the main character is stranded on a desert island. At first, he thinks he is alone. With a few supplies saved from his ship, he builds a house and a boat. He finds food and water to survive. He stays out of the hands of cannibals and rescues a man he calls Friday. For a man who had never lived in these circumstances before, Crusoe shows great resourcefulness in simply surviving. Eventually, he is rescued.

- The book *The Adventures of Huckleberry Finn* by Mark Twain is full of examples of resourcefulness. During a flood, Huck and a runaway slave named Jim get off an island by capturing a passing raft. They then escape a gang of robbers. When men come looking for Jim, Huck tells them the man on the raft has smallpox. They leave because they are afraid to catch the disease.

Resourceful characters in literature often survive in hard circumstances or escape from danger by using their wits. They use all the knowledge they have gained in their lives to get through. If you were put on a raft in a river or on a desert island, how would you survive?

> **"**Practical wisdom is only to be learned in the school of experience.**"**
> —Samuel Smiles, Political Reformer

Being Resourceful in Life

Consider this situation:

Hannah and her sister Sara were visiting Japan with their parents. Hannah was 17 and Sara was 10. While their parents were shopping in a department store, Hannah asked if she could take her sister across the street to the train station. She wanted to get a soda at the restaurant there. Although her mother was a little worried about having the girls go off on their own, her father reassured her, saying it was just across the street.

Hannah took Sara to the station, where they followed signs written in English and Japanese to get to the restaurant. It was downstairs and a few minutes' walk from the station's entrance. They ordered a couple of sodas and paid in the local money. Then they started back. At first, the signs going the other way were in English and Japanese, but at some point, the English stopped. People rushed past them in the busy station, and there was no information counter in sight. Afraid of getting lost, Hannah had an idea. The two girls backtracked to the last sign that had the name they needed to find in English on it. They studied the Japanese characters on the sign and then headed to the next sign. With the shapes of the strange letters in mind, they followed signs with those shapes and ended up at the right entrance.

Hannah thought of a way to get back without asking for help. They used information that was available, although it wasn't the type of information they might usually use. In a moment when some kids might panic, she figured out a solution. What would you do if you were lost in a foreign country?

Being Resourceful in Practice

Think of a problem you've given up on solving. Now consider it in a way you hadn't before. Could you find another person to help you? Could you use different materials to fix something or build something? Could you try a completely new approach?

Your solution may be a compromise, but would it get the job done? Try it. You might be surprised at the outcome and learn something in the process.

RESOURCEFULNESS CHECKLIST

- ◯ Don't be constrained by the way things have been done before.
- ◯ Look around at what's available to you. Then use it in clever ways to solve a problem.
- ◯ Stick with a problem until you figure it out.
- ◯ Try a new way of doing things.
- ◯ Consider all the possibilities.

Resourceful Role Models

Here are people with a reputation for being resourceful:

- Margaret Tobin Brown was born to a poor family in Colorado. She married a mining engineer who found a method of mining gold that made him rich. She helped start soup kitchens in their mining days and ran for Congress twice, never winning. In 1912, she was traveling in Europe and was a passenger on the Titanic. When the Titanic hit an iceberg and was sinking, she was one of the few people to keep her wits about her. She steered people into lifeboats before they were put into the water. After they were rescued, she organized survivor lists to be transmitted back to the United States.

- In 1927, Charles Lindbergh was the first person to fly over the Atlantic Ocean. He had challenges to overcome during the flight. He had so much fuel in the plane that taking off was difficult. He encountered fog and icy conditions and had to circle back and go around them. By spotting fishing boats in the water below, he found the coast of Ireland. He flew the plane low over land and shouted to people who helped direct him on his course with gestures. Lindbergh landed safely in Paris but had shown both courage and resourcefulness.

Resourceful people often stay calm in dangerous situations. They look for a way out and use what's at hand to save themselves and others. If you were in a dangerous situation, what would your first thoughts be? Could you look at the danger as a problem to solve? If you could, you might be a resourceful person.

What's in It for Me?

Consider these real-life consequences of being resourceful:

- You are able to get through difficult situations.

- You are someone people rely on in a crisis.

- You learn things from every situation and apply what you learn in the future.

- You will become known as a problem-solver at work and may receive financial or other rewards.

- People consider you to be clever.

Related Words to Explore

Here are some words related to the trait of being resourceful and to its opposite:

- Clever
- Self-reliant
- Independent
- Capable
- Ingenious

- Inventive
- Unimaginative
- Impractical
- Dependent

> **"**The greater the obstacle the more glory in overcoming it. **"**
>
> —Moliere, Actor and Dramatist

RESPECTFUL

Being respectful means honoring and being considerate of others. When you respect someone or something, you appreciate its uniqueness. You may be polite to people, but to really respect them, you have to look for aspects of them that you value.

In what ways are you respectful?

What Does It Mean to Be Respectful?

All things on earth have value and uniqueness. Learning to value each person or thing and to show respect is an important part of getting along in the world. You may not always understand or agree with others. Still, you should respect everyone's right to have his or her own opinions and beliefs.

Respect takes little effort, but it can make others feel good. Showing respect doesn't say that you agree with everything about a person. It says that you honor that person's right to be unique.

In what ways are you respectful to your family, friends, and others? How do you feel when people respect your feelings or beliefs?

Respectfulness through Time

Here are examples of people showing respect for each other in two cultures:

- In medieval times, chivalry was a code that governed the activities of knights in Europe. The knights' code stated that they should respect weaknesses and become a defender of them. This was especially true in the treatment of women. Although by our standards, women were not given much freedom in those days, chivalry taught a respect for women.

- In Japanese society, respect is a very highly held value. Respect is given based on several factors: gender, age, and position, for example. The Japanese language has different structures for words based on the position of a person to whom you are talking. In a Japanese family, each person has a specific role. Being rude or showing disrespect is usually frowned on in the Japanese culture.

Different cultures require respect for different things. What do you respect most?

> **"**It requires vision, initiative, patience, respect, persistence, courage, and faith to be a transforming leader.**"**
> —**Stephen Covey, Motivational Writer**

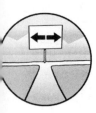

Being Respectful in Life

Consider this situation:

> *Miranda wasn't looking forward to the visit her 4-H club was going to make to the nursing home on Tyler Street. The kids were going to take their pets to visit the people. She thought the people there would be boring.*
>
> *On the day of the 4-H club's visit, Miranda wandered away from the rest of the group with her cat Spitfire under her arm. An elderly woman in a wheelchair called her over. "Young lady," she said, "may I pet your cat?" Miranda stayed and chatted for a while, and was amazed to find out the woman had been a lawyer, just like Miranda wanted to be. The woman told Miranda of a few important cases she had tried and some famous people she had worked with. She pointed out other people at the home who had been pilots or authors or musicians.*
>
> *By the time the group left, Miranda realized she had not had respect for these people when she arrived. From her visit, however, she had learned to respect that they had interesting and important life experiences.*

Do you know any older people? Have you really listened to them talk about their lives? You can find something to respect in all people, no matter what their age or occupation.

   Young Person's Character Education Handbook, © JIST Life

Being Respectful in Practice

Pick a person in your life, such as a parent or teacher, whom you respect. Make a list of the things about that person that you respect. Now look at others around you, and see if you can find at least one thing to respect about each person. It's likely that you will find that everybody you know has some trait worthy of respect, whether or not you noticed it before.

RESPECTFULNESS CHECKLIST

○ Look for the best in people.

○ Show courtesy and consideration to everybody you meet.

○ Have respect for yourself and your body by taking care of yourself.

○ Respect the differences that make each person unique.

○ Respect nature and the world around you.

❝Respect...is appreciation of the separateness of the other person, of the ways in which he or she is unique.**❞**
—**Annie Gottlieb, Actress**

Respectful Role Models

Here are people with a reputation for being respectful.

- Rachel Carson was a marine biologist who wrote several significant books about respect for nature and our environment. Her book *Silent Spring* exposed corporate abuses of the environment. She led the fight against use of a dangerous pesticide, DDT, by farmers. Though perhaps disrespectful of those who abused nature, Carson had a respect and love for our world. So her work to protect it makes Carson a most respectful person.

- Juliette Gordon Low, founder of the Girl Scouts, brought the concept of self-respect to girls all over America. Part of the Girl Scout law reads "to respect myself and others [and] respect authority." Lowe encouraged girls to develop their potential and gain skills to help them succeed. Her respect of others' abilities and potential makes her an excellent role model.

We can respect many things. We can respect other people, animals, nature, each others' beliefs, and ourselves. Respect means to show honor and consideration. We all hope others will respect us. Isn't it only fair that we respect them, too?

What's in It for Me?

Consider these real-life consequences of being respectful:

- You honor and value what is unique in everybody and everything.

- Others think of you as considerate and polite.

- In practicing respect, you learn to develop self-respect as well.

- Respect puts you on an even footing with every other creature. You are not better, nor worse.

Related Words to Explore

Here are some words related to the trait of being respectful and to its opposite:

- Deferential
- Reverent
- Polite
- Considerate

- Honorable
- Disrespectful
- Rude

RESPONSIBLE

Taking responsibility for your actions can be difficult. It may involve admitting when you make a mistake. It may mean following through on a promise even though you would rather not.

Are you a responsible person?

What Does It Mean to Be Responsible?

Being responsible means that you answer for your actions. If you say you will do something, you follow through on your promise. If you make a mistake, you admit it and take responsibility for the consequences.

As you grow older, you will get more freedom to act as you like. No teacher or parent will be around to make you be responsible. You will have to take responsibility for your own life and actions.

Consider these examples of being responsible:

- You promise to meet a friend after school to help move some boxes. You show up on time. You do the work you said you would do.

- You decide to set up the outdoor grill for a parent. As you drag it to the backyard, the wheel breaks off on a rock. You admit to your parent what happened and offer to help fix it.

- You ask a parent to buy you a puppy. You promise you will take care of it. Without anybody reminding you, you feed and walk the dog every day.

Responsibility through Time

Here are some examples of responsibility.

- President Harry Truman kept a sign on his desk. The sign said, "The buck stops here." This referred to the phrase, passing the buck, which means to pass on responsibility for something. He said, "You know, it's easy for the Monday morning quarterback to say what the coach should have done, after the game is over. But when the decision is up before you—and on my desk I have a motto which says 'The buck stops here.'—the decision has to be made." Truman did more than talk about responsibility. Before he became president, he owned a store in Missouri. In hard times, the store closed. Truman spent years paying back the money he owed people.

- An organization called Physicians for Social Responsibility was founded in 1961. The group of 24,000 members works to have nations stop the use of nuclear weapons. Members also work toward a healthier environment and an end to gun violence. The members volunteer their time and money to make changes. They do this because they believe they have a responsibility for others.

What do you feel responsible for in your life? Are you responsible for yourself, for what your government does, for what your friends do? Deciding what you should take responsibility for is part of figuring out who you are. The impact that you have on the world is related to the things for which you take responsibility.

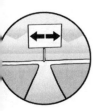

Being Responsible in Life

Consider this situation:

> *Mr. Herman was a new teacher at the school. Mike's best friend, Dylan, seemed to take an instant dislike to Mr. Herman.*
>
> *Dylan kept talking to Mike during class, even though Mr. Herman asked him to be quiet several times. Mike started to joke around with Dylan. Mr. Herman finally came over to the two and gave Dylan a blue slip, telling him to go to Mrs. McCarty's class for think time. As Dylan left the room, Mike tried to think what he should do.*

What would you do if you were Mike? He knew that he had been talking in class also, even though Dylan started it. Should he admit to Mr. Herman that he was talking, too, and take his punishment? Because Dylan "started it," should Mike let him take all the responsibility? If we join in with bad behavior, is that as bad as starting it? What could Mike gain by taking responsibility for his behavior? What could he lose?

> **"** You cannot evade the responsibility of tomorrow by evading it today. **"**
>
> —Abraham Lincoln, U.S. President

Being Responsible in Practice

Take responsibility for something in your life. If you have just made a mistake, admit it. Take responsibility for a project you are doing. Have you made a promise to somebody but put off doing what you promised? Try following through on something that somebody expects of you. For example, does a parent constantly remind you to take out the garbage? This week, do it before he or she gets a chance to ask.

How does it feel to take responsibility for something? Did you get punished? Did somebody thank you for what you did? Use the following checklist to measure your sense of responsibility.

RESPONSIBILITY CHECKLIST

○ Follow through on promises.

○ Take responsibility for actions of others when you are in charge.

○ Admit when you make a mistake.

○ Don't blame others for your actions.

○ Don't say you will do something that you do not intend to do.

○ Do the things you say you will do without anybody telling you to.

" *The price of greatness is responsibility.* **"**
—Winston Churchill, British Prime Minister

Responsible Role Models

Here are some people in various walks of life. Each has a reputation for taking responsibility.

- Nathan Hale fought in the American Revolution. He was caught near New York City. He would not lie about his identity. When the British learned who he was, they sentenced him to hang. Some say Hale took responsibility for his actions as a spy against the British. Others say that those who lied about their identities could be hung as spies. Maybe Hale thought he could get off the charge of spying by not lying about his identity. Whatever his reasons, he took responsibility for his actions. This gave new energy to the cause of the revolution. Today, we remember Hale as a hero.

- The famous story about the cherry tree tells how George Washington took responsibility for his actions. Supposedly, young George chopped down a tree. His father discovered this and got angry. George stepped forward and admitted he had cut down the tree. Nobody knows what happened to George, or even if the story is true. In later years, Washington took on the responsibility of leading the army in the American Revolution. He then became our first president.

- Emma Goldman was a feminist (somebody who fights for women's rights) who lived from 1869 to 1940. She spoke out for women's freedoms. She even went to prison for her actions. She also traveled to Russia and Spain to fight against dictatorships (governments where one person tells everybody else what to do). Goldman put herself in danger to fight for causes she believed in. She took responsibility for her beliefs.

What's in It for Me?

Consider these real-life consequences of being responsible or not being responsible:

- People who are irresponsible are not trusted. They may get away with being irresponsible, but others will have the sense that they are not dependable.

- Responsible people are admired by others. They often become leaders. Recognition, awards, and sometimes higher pay can come with responsibility.

- Employers are unlikely to promote people they cannot depend on. They will not give responsibility to those who can't handle responsibility. Your work will never be very challenging or rewarding if you are not responsible.

Related Words to Explore

Here are some words related to the trait of responsibility and to its opposite, irresponsibility:

- Dependable
- Accountable
- Reliable
- Liable
- Answerable

- Honorable
- Evasive
- Untrustworthy

SELF-CONFIDENT

Self-confident people think they can accomplish almost anything they take on. They try things others hesitate to try. They have faith in their own abilities. They also know that the price of not trying to achieve something is higher than the price of failing.

Do you have confidence in your own abilities?

What Does It Mean to Be Self-Confident?

There is an important difference between self-confidence and pride. Self-confident people feel they have what it takes to try, even if they don't succeed. People who have too much pride think that they will always succeed or that they are better than other people.

We all have strengths and weaknesses. Self-confidence means knowing what you are good at and what you are not good at. Self-confident people know a secret: When you try and fail, you find that having survived failure gives you more confidence that you'll do better next time.

What are you self-confident about? What do you know you can do well? Are you willing to tackle a new challenge, knowing that you have what it takes to succeed? Do you know self-confident people?

Self-Confidence through Time

There are examples of self-confidence in history and poetry:

- Joan of Arc led an army with confidence born of her spiritual beliefs. Theodosia Garrison wrote a poem called "The Soul of Joan of Arc" that describes Joan of Arc's confidence. Other leaders such as Napoleon have shown great self-confidence in leading troops because of their particular skill at strategy. Fighting in a war or fighting for a cause often takes great self-confidence because the stakes are high.

- In his poem "Paul Revere's Ride," Henry Wadsworth Longfellow wrote of Revere's ride to Lexington, Massachusetts, to warn people of the approach of British troops. In this last stanza of the poem, Revere rode in defiance, not in fear and, we assume, with no small amount of self-confidence in himself and his mission.

> **“**He who has lost confidence can lose nothing more. **”**
>
> **—Boiste, Lexicographer**

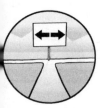

Being Self-Confident in Life

Consider this situation:

Juliana had transferred to Franklin Middle School mid-year. When tryouts for the school spring musical were announced, she knew that she wanted to audition. She had learned that Marianne was the lead in the school play last year and that Marianne was a favorite of the director. Still, Juliana had been cast as the lead in a community theater play last year in her hometown and felt she could compete with Marianne. In any case, she loved being in plays and knew trying out was worth the risk.

When the day of the auditions came, Juliana had studied the score for the play and felt confident that she had a chance to succeed. Marianne gave a very good audition and sang beautifully. Then it was Juliana's turn. Without hesitation, she went up on the stage, gave her music to the piano player, and began to sing.

Did Juliana get the part? Does it matter? She wanted to play the part, and she tried for it. She would have been very happy to get it, but she would not feel that she had no talent or should never try again if she didn't. Self-confidence means that defeat doesn't get you down. You know what you can do, and you keep at it. Is that what you do in your life? What would be the rewards of that kind of attitude?

> **❝**You must do the thing that you think you cannot do.**❞**
>
> —Eleanor Roosevelt, Humanitarian and Writer

Being Self-Confident in Practice

Have you hesitated to try something because you lacked confidence? Try to tackle this task feeling that you have what it takes to succeed. If you fail, you may learn something. But if you never try, you can never hope to succeed.

SELF-CONFIDENCE CHECKLIST

- ◯ Try things that are challenging, knowing that you have what it takes to succeed.
- ◯ If you fail, don't let failure stop you from trying again.
- ◯ Look on the positive side of things.
- ◯ Don't let fear rule your choices in life.
- ◯ Know your strengths and use them boldly.

Self-Confident Role Models

Here are people known for having a self-confident attitude.

- Eleanor Roosevelt was the wife of President Franklin D. Roosevelt. In her younger years, she was molded by her times in thinking that women had no role in politics. But as the president's wife, she spoke out for women's rights in the workplace, fair labor conditions, and civil rights. This strong, intelligent woman was not taught to be self-confident. She learned self-confidence.

- Mark Twain showed self-confidence. By age 16, he had worked as a reporter and Western Union agent. At age 21, he talked a steamboat pilot on the Mississippi River into taking him on as an apprentice and received his steamboat pilot's license at age 23. He went west and prospected for gold and then took a job as a reporter. He arranged to be a correspondent for his newspaper aboard a ship headed for Russia and the Middle East. Twain went on to hold many more jobs and to publish many books. It is clear that Twain didn't hesitate to jump into the next experience, confident that he could tackle it.

Not all self-confident people are born that way. Some people learn through failure that the worst that can happen is not all that bad. This gives them courage to be more confident in the future. Is there something in your life that has caused you to become more self-confident?

What's in It for Me?

Consider these real-life consequences of being self-confident:

- There are few things that you hesitate to try.

- You can inspire others to be more confident.

- You don't let a single failure get you down but have faith in your overall ability to get things done.

- People see you as a strong leader or teacher.

- Self-confident people can find great success in business or other fields.

Related Words to Explore

Here are some words related to the trait of being self-confident and to its opposite:

- Self-assured
- Self-possessed
- Poised
- Insecure

- Shy
- Timid
- Reserved

> **"**You have to have confidence in your ability, and then be tough enough to follow through.**"**
> —**Rosalynn Carter, Former First Lady**

SELF-DISCIPLINED

People with self-discipline set their own rules and follow them. If they have to be someplace on time, they get there. If they are studying a hobby, they make time to practice and read. Sometimes people are self-disciplined about one thing, such as practicing the piano. However, they may be less self-disciplined about other things, such as not eating too many desserts.

In what ways are you self-disciplined?

What Does It Mean to Be Self-Disciplined?

Self-disciplined people control their impulses and focus their energy to accomplish things without anybody telling them to. They apply rules for themselves to get where they want to go. Self-disciplined people might be good at saving money, losing weight, or learning how to dance or speak a foreign language. They set goals and establish routines that help them achieve those goals.

We are not self-disciplined in every aspect of our lives. But when it is important to reach a goal, self-disciplined people draw on an inner strength.

Are you are self-disciplined in a certain area of your life? Do you make yourself do your homework without being reminded? Do you work hard at sports or music or a hobby? Perhaps you are self-disciplined!

Self-Discipline through Time

You often see self-discipline in the arts, for example:

- Musicians have to practice long hours, even after they become successful. Classical concert pianists might practice six or more hours a day. Opera singers work for years to train their voices and to learn to sing works written in several languages. Jazz musicians take every opportunity to work with other musicians and learn through improvising.

- Dancers have to discipline their bodies. They have to practice movements and leaps carefully to avoid injury. Dancers may have a career for only 20 years because dancing is so physically demanding.

Do you love doing something enough that you are willing to spend the time and effort to become really good at it? Do you like to dance, act, or sing? Do you love playing sports? The people who become successful in these fields have to be very self-disciplined.

> **"**Lasting accomplishment ... is achieved through a long, slow climb and self-discipline.**"**
> —Helen Hayes, Actress

Being Self-Disciplined in Life

Consider this situation:

> *Karla wanted to get accepted by the regional synchronized swimming team. Getting on the team meant long hours of practice after school and on weekends. Karla knew she was a good swimmer, so she told her father she wanted to do anything it took to make the team.*
>
> *Every day after school Karla practiced for two hours at the YWCA. She ran for an hour every morning before school to build up her leg muscles. Her father told her she must also keep up her schoolwork, so she spent a few hours on homework every day. Often she had to skip a movie with friends or a trip to the mall so she could get in more practice.*
>
> *Karla sometimes went to bed exhausted after a long day. Still, she had a goal in mind and worked hard to get there. Her father never had to remind her to practice because she disciplined herself to do what she had to do to meet her goal.*

Have you ever made yourself work hard to achieve something? Has something ever been important enough to you that you did what you had to do to make it happen? Although self-discipline is hard, it often has great rewards.

Being Self-Disciplined in Practice

Think of something you've always wanted to do but felt that you lacked the self-discipline to achieve. Perhaps you want to learn a skill. Or perhaps you want to exercise more. Set specific goals and figure out how to get there. Find ways to check your own progress. Find ways to reward yourself when you succeed or motivate yourself when you fail.

SELF-DISCIPLINE CHECKLIST

- ◯ Set goals and do what it takes to reach them.
- ◯ Control yourself so that sudden urges don't undermine your overall goal.
- ◯ Imagine what it would be like if you achieved what you want.
- ◯ Don't let things or people distract you from what you want to achieve.
- ◯ Set routines that help you control your behavior.

> **"** As you become successful, you will need a great deal of self-discipline not to lose your sense of balance, humility, and commitment. **"**
>
> —H. Ross Perot, Industrialist

Self-Disciplined Role Models

Here are some people from various walks of life. Each has a reputation for self-discipline.

- Lon Chaney was an actor in the era of silent movies. He grew up with deaf parents. As a result, he learned early to show his feelings through expressions and movement rather than through words. To play the lead in *The Hunchback of Notre Dame,* he wore a harness and artificial hump weighing more than 50 pounds. The pain it caused him allowed him to give a realistic performance as the pain-wrenched character.

- Dancer Mikhail Baryshnikov began a dancing career at the age of 15, always striving for perfection. During a dance tour in Canada, he defected from the Soviet Union. He has taken on many forms of dance, from classical ballet to Broadway musicals to jazz. A professional dance career demands incredible physical and mental self-discipline, of which Baryshnikov seems to have had plenty.

- Vince Lombardi was a football coach who expected 110 percent effort from his players. He himself often worked 17-hour days. He held very intensive training camps for his players but worked equally hard and promised his players they would be champions. He led the Green Bay Packers to nine consecutive winning seasons. Lombardi helped the men he coached succeed by instilling self-discipline.

What's in It for Me?

Consider these real-life consequences of being self-disciplined:

- You can achieve your goals in life.

- You can make plans that get you where you want to go.

- People will respect your ability to get things done and not be distracted.

- You may master difficult skills.

- At work, self-disciplined people are seen as achievers and often promoted or rewarded.

Related Words to Explore

Here are some words related to the trait of being self-disciplined and to its opposite:

- Abstemious
- Moderate
- Temperate
- Self-controlled
- Restraint

- Willpower
- Strength of will
- Self-indulgent
- Undisciplined
- Lazy

> **"**With self-discipline, most anything is possible.**"**
> —Theodore Roosevelt, U.S. President

SELF-RELIANT

Self-reliant people are confident about tackling projects on their own. They don't rely on other people to help them out. In fact, they often prefer to go it alone. They depend on their own intelligence, skills, and determination to get by.

Have you known many self-reliant people?

What Does It Mean to Be Self-Reliant?

There is an important difference between self-confidence and self-reliance, though they are often companion traits. Self-confident people believe they can succeed at whatever they take on. Self-reliant people feel they can do things without help. They find within themselves what's needed to get through in most situations.

Self-reliant people may get along well with people and work well with others. If they have to handle a project alone, however, they don't hesitate to. They trust their instincts and count on their skills to get things done.

Are you self-reliant? If you were given the choice between doing a school project alone or with a partner, which would you choose? If you were in a strange situation, would you feel confident that you could get through it on your own?

Self-Reliance through Time

There have been many examples of self-reliance in society. Here are a few:

- In home schooling, parents take on the education of their children themselves. They do not rely on the public or private school system. Prior to 1900, many children were educated at home or had no formal education. Public schools started only about 150 years ago. Now people who are dissatisfied with school systems that are underfunded or overcrowded are taking education into their own hands. This family self-reliance takes cooperation and effort from everybody involved.

- Some people don't like to rely on the government or businesses. They don't have TVs or dishwashers. These people live "off the grid," meaning they don't hook up their homes to public utilities such as electricity, water, telephones, or cable TV. They may use a generator for electricity or do without. Some of these people are concerned that the systems most people rely on may collapse or fail. For that reason, they are happier relying on themselves.

People decide to do without others' support for various reasons. Sometimes they are loners. Other times they distrust a system and think they can do better by not depending on it. Yet others feel greater reward if they achieve things on their own. Do you prefer to do something on your own? Perhaps in that area of your life, you are self-reliant.

Being Self-Reliant in Life

Consider this situation:

> *Caleb loved to ride his bike. One weekend a dog ran out in front of him, and he fell, damaging the bike. He walked it home, put it in the garage, and didn't say a thing to his foster father. The next weekend Caleb spent a few hours trying to fix the bike. He had to walk to his friend Joe's to borrow a wrench. He spent time on the computer looking up the manufacturer's manual online. After figuring out how to fix the bike, he struggled with straightening a bent fender.*
>
> *Toward the end of the day, Caleb's foster father came home. When Caleb told him about the bike and how he had fixed it himself, his foster father was surprised because he owned a bike shop and could have fixed the bike for Caleb quickly.*
>
> *"It felt good to figure it all out on my own," said Caleb.*

Is it sometimes more fun to figure something out yourself than to ask for help? Does it feel good to work through a problem or process without help? Self-reliance can help you feel good about yourself. The more things you accomplish alone, the more self-reliant you become.

Being Self-Reliant in Practice

All by yourself, try doing something that you usually do with the help of others. Make sure you have what you need to succeed, and then tackle the project. What surprises did you encounter? Did you feel that it was easier when you had others' help? Did you feel a greater sense of accomplishment from completing the task all by yourself?

SELF-RELIANCE CHECKLIST

○ Recognize tasks you can do without help, and take them on.

○ Recognize and appreciate your own skills and abilities.

○ Enjoy the satisfaction of accomplishing things on your own.

○ Don't be afraid to go it alone.

○ Know when you need help, but don't underestimate your own talents.

Self-Reliant Role Models

Here are people active in sports and known for a self-reliant attitude.

- Ellen MacArthur became the top solo sailor in the world in 2005. She sailed alone for almost 72 days, setting a solo around-the-world record. Though only 28 years old and petite, MacArthur has succeeded in a sport that requires strength for changing sails and pulling rigging. She seems to delight in solo sailing over team sailing, having also won an around-the-world solo sailing race in 2000.

- The people who compete in Alaska's Iditarod dogsled race have to be self-reliant to succeed. Although they have the help of their dog teams, no humans are there to help them in the grueling race across icy lands. A Norwegian firefighter, Robert Sorlie, won the race in 2003 and 2005, only the sixth person in history to win twice. Sorlie had to drive his dog team over 1,150 miles of rugged terrain in freezing conditions.

Sometimes we discover in tough times that we are more self-reliant than we thought. If we stay in control, use all the resources at hand, and do the best we can without calling for help, we are self-reliant. Some people seek situations that pit them against nature or another challenge. Have you ever been in that kind of situation? What did you do?

> **"**The spirit of self-help is the root of all genuine growth in the individual.**"**
> —**Samuel Smiles, Political Reformer**

What's in It for Me?

Consider these real-life consequences of being self-reliant:

- There are few things that you hesitate to try.
- You can inspire others to appreciate their own capabilities.
- You develop skills that help you take care of yourself in many situations.
- People see you as a strong person who can get things done.
- Self-reliant people can often find great success in careers that demand that they go it alone.

Related Words to Explore

Here are some words related to the trait of being self-reliant and to its opposite:

- Self-sufficient
- Independent
- Self-possessed
- Self-contained
- Autonomous
- Needy
- Insecure
- Dependent

SENSE OF HUMOR

Having a sense of humor means that you can see the funny side of things. You might be good at making jokes or making funny faces. A sense of humor gives you a way to get through tough times and make the most of good times.

Do you have a good sense of humor?

What Does It Mean to Have a Sense of Humor?

People have varying degrees of a sense of humor, and they laugh at different types of humor. What's funny to one person may not be funny to another. However, people with a good sense of humor tend to see the bright side. They like to laugh and make others laugh.

Often humor pokes fun at the things that all people do. When people hear a comedian talk about how he loses his keys, they laugh because they lose their keys and know how he feels. But making fun of the human condition and making fun of people aren't the same thing: One shows a sense of humor; the other may show meanness.

Do you look for the fun in situations? Do you look for what you can laugh at rather than what is wrong? If you do, you may have a good sense of humor.

A Sense of Humor through Time

Here are some examples of a sense of humor in different comedy styles:

- Slapstick uses physical "jokes." If you have ever seen movies with the Three Stooges or the Marx Brothers, you have seen examples of slapstick. Silent movies in the early 1900s used slapstick because there was no dialogue to convey humor. Slapstick is used today in comedy movies and plays, though much less than in the era of silent films. Slapstick is related to another comedy form, the Italian commedia dell'arte. In these short plays, a character whacks others with a stick. The word *slapstick* comes from the slapping motion of this stick in the earlier form of comedy.

- Political humor pokes fun at politicians and governments but also gets people thinking about serious issues. Satire is one form of humor that started in literature and is used in political humor today. Satirists ridicule their subject, often by making exaggerated comparisons. When you hear a satirist, rather than laughing out loud as you might with a slapstick performer, you may shake you head, smile, and say, "Sad, but true."

Different kinds of humor work at different times. Humor poking fun at institutions can help to improve our world. But in difficult times, people may just want to be entertained. For that reason, you will find more straight comedy at times of national stress. Are you sometimes in the mood for one kind of humor over another? Why?

Having a Sense of Humor in Life

Consider this situation:

Breanna was planning to surprise her parents at their anniversary party. She wanted to play their favorite song on her clarinet. She practiced every afternoon before her mother got home from work. Her brother, Theo, hated clarinet. He walked around with his fingers in his ears. She told him to go out in the yard if he hated it that much and kept practicing. The day of the party arrived, and she was excited about the surprise.

When Breanna went upstairs to assemble her clarinet, she discovered that her brother had hidden it. At first, she was angry; then she thought of a plan. She went downstairs and got everybody's attention. "I was going to play our parents' favorite song on my clarinet," Breanna announced. "But Theo decided he'd rather sing the song for you. Theo?" Her brother looked mortified. Everybody knew he had the worst singing voice in the world. Her brother started laughing at the private joke, and she and her parents joined in. After a minute, Theo reached behind the couch and handed the clarinet to Breanna. Smiling, she assembled it and played the song.

Breanna and her brother showed that they had senses of humor. Instead of letting a disappointment get her angry, Breanna turned the situation around. Instead of letting Breanna embarrass him, Theo was able to laugh at himself and make up for what he had done. Laughter is often a good replacement for anger, revenge, or frustration. Try it yourself!

Having a Sense of Humor in Practice

The next time you are disappointed, try to consider the humor in the situation. Perhaps you can change the mood of people by making them laugh instead of brooding over a problem. Remember that laughter should be appropriate and should not be at the expense of any person.

SENSE OF HUMOR CHECKLIST

○ Look on the bright side of things.

○ Don't let things get you down. Find ways to learn something about human nature from every experience.

○ Don't take life too seriously. Learn to bounce back from difficult times.

○ Use humor to help others cope with difficulties.

○ Watch people and yourself, and find the things in human nature that connect us all.

> **"**The humorist does not laugh so much at mankind as he invites mankind to laugh at itself.**"**
> —Peter De Vries, Author

Sense of Humor Role Models

Here are some people who have shown a sense of humor.

- Mark Twain, described in "self-confident" on page 242, was a humorist who wrote novels with colorful characters. He had a knack for drawing funny pictures of the human condition with his words. Twain had a good sense of humor. When a newspaper incorrectly published a story that Twain had died, Twain said, "The reports of my death have been greatly exaggerated."

- People often think of Alfred Hitchcock as a director of suspense films. However, many of his films show humor, and some are categorized as comedies. Some of the humor in his films is called *black humor* because it is about something morbid or dark.

Humor is often connected to the human condition. Human flaws and behavior, and subjects that we find hard to deal with such as death, are often the subject of humor. Laughing at difficulties or at what we recognize in our own lives can be a way to come to grips with our lives. What makes you laugh? Does laughter make tough times easier to deal with?

> **"**Humor is the shock absorber of life: it helps us take the blows.**"**
>
> —Peggy Noonan, Political Columnist

What's in It for Me?

Humorous people can reap many benefits. For example, they can

- Be socially popular because people enjoy being around them.
- Help themselves and others to get through tragedies.
- Gain fame as an entertainer or writer.
- Be respected for being positive when times are rough.

Related Words to Explore

Here are some words related to the trait of having a sense of humor and to its opposite:

- Comic
- Witty
- Funny
- Hilarious
- Joking
- Jesting

- Flippant
- Serious
- Solemn
- Somber
- Stern

SENSITIVE

Sensitive people are alert to what's going on around them. They may notice how people around them are feeling more than others do. They may be touched by pain, kindness, beauty, and hardship more than most. If people are too sensitive, they can become overwhelmed by life. If they are not sensitive enough, they can be mean to others.

Are there things that affect you strongly? If so, you are probably sensitive to those things.

What Does It Mean to Be Sensitive?

People are not always sensitive to everything. Some people are sensitive to other people's feelings. Others are sensitive to art or beautiful objects. Some sensitive people can get their own feelings hurt easily.

Being sensitive simply means that you react to or are affected by things. Being sensitive helps you appreciate the world you live in. Sadly, all of us become insensitive to certain things as we gain experience. However, this insensitivity can be useful in helping us to survive. The important point to keep in mind is that sensitivity must be a balance between being open to experience and being too deeply affected by it.

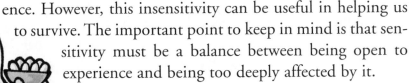

Sensitivity through Time

Here are some examples of sensitivity in nature.

- Owls have incredibly sensitive eyes. They can easily sense both light and movement. Their eyes are very large, providing up to 5 percent of their body weight. Owls can see things in three dimensions, which is unusual for birds and many animals. They use their sensitive eyes to see prey in the dark, because they are active at night. To protect their eyes, they have three eyelids.

- Bats have the ability to use a kind of sonar. When they make a sound, depending on how long the echo of the sound takes to come back, they can sense how far away an object is. Their hearing is very sharp. Some believe they can hear the flutter of a bird or insect's wings and compute the flight speed of their prey from that sound.

Many animals and birds use sensitivity to something—sounds, smells, or movement—to help them survive. Have you ever had a dog that could hear a person coming up to your house long before you could? People use their senses to pick up information about others and the world. We can be sensitive to how our words affect people by watching their reactions. Sensitive people learn by observing how to treat people so they do not upset them.

> **❝**It is usually the imagination that is wounded first, rather than the heart; it being much more sensitive.**❞**
> —Henry David Thoreau, Essayist

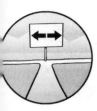

Being Sensitive in Life

Consider this situation:

On Monday, Carolyn came to school thinking about her swim meet the following day. When she turned the corner to go to her locker, she noticed a small group of students gathered in the hallway. They were whispering and looking down the other end of the hall.

"Look, he's stuck!" said Marilee. As she came closer, Carolyn noticed that the person they were talking about was a new student who sat in a wheelchair. He was trying to enter a classroom down the hall, but his chair wheel had caught on the edge of the door. As he wheeled his chair backward, he glanced down the hall at the group looking at him.

"Oh, be quiet," said Carolyn to her friends, as she moved away from them and approached the boy. "Hi, I'm Carolyn," she said when she reached the boy in the chair. "Can I help?" He thanked her, and she shifted his chair and helped him get into the classroom.

Carolyn was the only one of her friends who was sensitive to the feelings of the new boy in school. Have you ever been sensitive to somebody else's feelings? Have you been hurt when people made fun of you? Perhaps you are a sensitive person.

> **❝**The more alert and sensitive we are to our own needs, the more loving and generous we can be toward others.**❞**
>
> —Eda LeShan, Author

Being Sensitive in Practice

For one day, try to be aware of how people react to what you say and do. During the day, did you hurt anybody's feelings? Did you sense something about somebody you had never realized before? Did your sensitivity help you avoid hurting somebody?

SENSITIVITY CHECKLIST

◯ Listen to people and be aware of their feelings.

◯ Don't say or do things without thinking about how they might affect other people.

◯ Be responsive to things around you.

◯ Combine your ability to be aware of what's around you with other traits such as compassion or courage and see what happens.

◯ Try to find ways to connect with other people and understand what makes them happy or sad.

Sensitive Role Models

Here are two people who are known for their sensitivity:

- Lord Byron was born to a poor family. Because he had a deformed foot, he was very sensitive about his handicap. At the age of 10, he inherited a title and money from his great uncle. He began to write poetry and eventually became famous. His poems spoke of love and foreign lands. His romantic vision of the world caused him to repeatedly fall in love. His poems reflect his sensitive nature.

- John Edward is a world-famous psychic medium who claims to be sensitive to communications from people who have "crossed over," that is, people who have died. He appears on television and gives lectures where he helps people communicate with their friends and relatives. As a child, he knew things about his family that nobody had told him. How he does what he does is a mystery, but he appears to be sensitive to things the average person cannot feel.

What's in It for Me?

Sensitive people can reap many benefits. For example, they can

- Be alert to others' feelings and help them cope with hard times.

- Help themselves and others to get through tragedies.

- Notice things other people miss and appreciate things others don't respond to.

- Be respected for being responsive to the things and people around them.

Related Words to Explore

Here are some words related to the trait of being sensitive and to its opposite:

- Aware
- Perceptive
- Insightful
- Responsive
- Intuitive

- Thick-skinned
- Insensitive
- Indifferent
- Callous

> **❝**All sensitive people agree that there is a peculiar emotion provoked by works of art.**❞**
> —Clive Bell, Art Critic

TEAM PLAYER

A team is any group of people working toward a common goal. Examples are sports teams and teams that work together on projects. People who know how to behave when working with others in a team are called team players. They fit in with the group and do what's required to reach the common goal.

When you are part of a team, how do you behave?

What Does It Mean to Be a Team Player?

Being a team player means that you don't try to outshine everybody else. You don't go off on your own. Instead, you work with other people. You keep everybody informed and don't try to grab the glory for successes. Team players don't blame others on the team for mistakes. They try to help each other.

Being a team player isn't always easy. If somebody else on the team ruins something you've been working on, you have to stay calm and friendly. If another person on the team doesn't do his or her part, you have to keep your team spirit. A team not only has to do the work, but it has to keep the team relationship healthy.

Usually, no one person can achieve the things a team can because a team combines many perspectives and skills. When a team reaches its goal, whether by winning a game or producing a play together, team members can share in the rewards and recognition.

Team Players through Time

There are many examples of successful team efforts in the world, for example:

- The Olympics is an excellent example of the paradox (or puzzle) of team spirit. It is a huge sporting event that brings people together. However, the teams compete against each other, working on opposite sides. The Olympics brings together many countries, but it causes people to be divided as they cheer on their sides. One motivation of team players is to make their group the best and beat something: a challenge, another team, another company, or another country. When you join a team, consider what you are for and what you are against!

- The Manhattan Project was a combined effort of many people to develop the atomic bomb that played a big part in ending World War II. Three separate facilities were set up. Chemists, physicists, and physicians were brought together. They looked at ways to create the atomic reaction, ways to deliver it, and the effects of radiation. The outcome of this project was bombs. However, teamwork was required to coordinate these many researchers in secrecy.

Being a team player means you further the goals of the team. Being a team player is a good skill to cultivate, but carefully choose the teams you will play or work on.

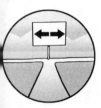

Being a Team Player in Life

Consider this situation:

> *Rowen loved to ride his bike. When a bicycle-racing club was formed at his school, he joined immediately. Mr. Hancock was the teacher in charge. He explained the rules for bicycle racing the first day.*
>
> *In a race, the bicyclist who comes in first on the last lap is the winner. Even if somebody else is ahead for the rest of the course, that person won't win if he's not first in the last lap. For that reason, the team members work together to make sure the best rider doesn't become tired during the race. They do that by riding ahead of him, protecting him from the wind so he needs less energy to move forward.*
>
> *Rowen went home and thought about what he had heard. Did he want to spend time and energy in a sport where he might seldom win, although he was a good rider? Could he feel that a winner on his team represented a win for the whole team? After thinking it over, Rowen decided not to stay with the club.*

Would you have made the same decision as Rowen? If your efforts help somebody else to shine, would you participate? Think of a play in which all the people work hard backstage so a few actors get the applause. Why do people do this? Do you think they feel that some part of the applause is for them? Would you feel that way?

   Young Person's Character Education Handbook, © JIST Life

Being a Team Player in Practice

Pick an activity in which you must function as part of a team. It might be rehearsing a concert or play, a sports event, or political action. Figure out your role in the group, and stick to it. Help people who need your help. Focus on the goal, not on yourself. If you succeed in doing these things, you're a team player!

TEAM PLAYER CHECKLIST

○ Consider the good of the group.

○ Focus on the goal at hand rather than personal glory.

○ Do the piece of the work you have been assigned, rather than taking over the work of others.

○ If others ask you for help, give it.

○ Respect the leader of your team.

"The important thing to recognize is that it takes a team, and the team ought to get credit for the wins and the losses. Successes have many fathers, failures have none."
—Philip Caldwell, Chief Executive Officer, Ford Motor Company

Team Player Role Models

Here are some people who have a reputation for being a team player:

- Lou Gehrig was a baseball legend remembered for acting more like a regular team member than a star. X rays show that he broke bones in his hands 17 times over the years. Yet, he continued to play, not wanting to let down the team. When he contracted a fatal disease and gave a farewell speech, he said about his team, "Look at these grand men. Which of you wouldn't consider it the highlight of your career just to associate with them for one day?" In the speech, he went on to honor opposing teams and his family, rather than focus on himself.

- Serena and Venus Williams are not only sisters, they are tennis champions. They practice together and sometimes play together in doubles competitions. They even play against each other. When they compete and one wins and the other loses, they support each other. Together with their parents and trainer, they seem to form a team that works for the success of the family, not one sister over the other.

- Pierre and Marie Curie were scientists who worked together on the discovery of radium. Pierre allowed Marie to use his laboratory, but as her work progressed, he abandoned his work to help her. They shared the work, each covering certain tasks. They were jointly awarded the Nobel Prize. When her husband was killed in an accident, Marie took over his professorship and raised funds for an institution in his memory.

What's in It for Me?

Consider these real-life consequences of being a team player:

- You can help to accomplish important things.

- You can add your talents to those of others to create bigger things than you could create alone.

- You are seen as cooperative.

- You know how to get along with others.

- Employers consider team players to be great assets.

Related Words to Explore

Here are some words related to the trait of being a team player and to its opposite:

- Cooperative
- Supportive
- Accommodating
- Collaborative
- Sharing

- Helpful
- Uncooperative
- Isolated
- Independent

> "Never doubt that a small group of thoughtful, committed citizens can change the world. Indeed, it is the only thing that ever has."
>
> —Margaret Mead, Anthropologist

THOROUGH

Thorough people never stop short of finishing a task. They never skip steps or do something halfway. Instead, thorough people make sure they do things well and don't let any details slip.

Is there an area of your life in which you are thorough?

What Does It Mean to Be Thorough?

People who want to be sure a job is well done are thorough. They cover all the steps in a process. They also double-check that things they are responsible for happen correctly. Thorough people pride themselves on doing a good job and never take shortcuts.

Although thoroughness isn't a glamorous trait, it is important. Thorough people do a good job and are people you can depend on. In certain fields, such as medicine, law, and science, being thorough can make the difference between success and failure.

In what ways are you thorough?

> **❝** If you would thoroughly know anything, teach it to others. **❞**
> —Tryon Edwards, Theologian and Editor

Thoroughness through Time

Here are two examples of situations that require thoroughness:

- The Human Genome Project was a 13-year assignment run by the U.S. Department of Energy and the National Institutes of Health. The project identified all the 20,000 to 25,000 genes in the human body that determine each individual's makeup. To do this, the people involved had to determine the chemical sequences of 3 billion chemical base pairs. They had to identify and store a lot of information. They couldn't skip a few genes. They had to be thorough in their work to get the complete picture of what makes up a human being.

- Making a fine musical instrument takes a thorough person because any mistake can change the sound it produces. In the 1600s, Augustus Stradivarius made violins that still are considered the best violins in the world. He was a fine craftsman whose violins give a unique tone. The almost 700 Stradivarius violins in the world each are worth a fortune. To this day, nobody has reproduced the process he used to create the best violins in the world.

Scientists, craftsmen, and others who work to reach the perfect result have to take the time to do things right. They have to be thorough. Facts have to be checked and rechecked. Measurements have to be exact.

Do you have the patience to do a thorough job in some area of your life?

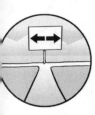

Being Thorough in Life

Consider this situation:

The drama class project was to create some kind of entertainment based on the life of a famous entertainer. The teacher divided the class into teams of four students. Kerry's team was assigned a famous singer.

The other teams did a little research on the Internet. Then they put together short plays or songs about the life of their entertainer. Kerry insisted her group go further.

Kerry and her group found a fan club Web site for the singer. They posted a message about their assignment in a discussion area, asking people to share their favorite story about him. They even found an e-mail address for the singer. They sent him an e-mail asking him if he'd mind answering some questions about how he got started and his favorite music. To their surprise, he answered the e-mail.

Kerry's team didn't stop there. They found a book in the library about the blues, which the singer had said was his biggest influence. Finally, they put together their skit, using famous blues musicians to narrate the piece, and little bits of what the singer had shared with them put to his music. Because they were so thorough, their teacher gave them the highest grade in the class.

 Young Person's Character Education Handbook, © JIST Life

Being Thorough in Practice

If you tend to gloss over things and do them quickly in an area of your life, take the time to get things right. If you rush through your math homework, take your time and do every problem. If you skip band rehearsals, put in a little extra practice. What are the rewards? What did you give up to be more thorough?

THOROUGHNESS CHECKLIST

- ○ Check things at every step to make sure they are correct.
- ○ Don't skip steps in a process to get it done quickly.
- ○ Find methods that help you remember every detail.
- ○ Verify your results.
- ○ Don't rush things; take the time to get things right.

> **"** I never failed once. It just happened to be a 2,000 step process. **"**
> —Thomas Edison, Inventor

Thorough Role Models

Here are two scientists known for being thorough.

- Dr. Donald Henderson led the World Health Organization in a fight against the deadly disease smallpox. He and his team had to work with every country in the world to find and treat smallpox outbreaks. They had to give shots to vaccinate every person in an infected area to stop the spread of the disease. In October 1977, Henderson and his team eliminated smallpox from the world, and it has never returned.

- Edmund Halley was a scientist in the 1600s. In 1695, Halley began to study the orbits of comets. He created a new theory of how comets orbit our earth. That theory allowed him to calculate the return of one comet, now called Halley's Comet. Though he had been dead for 15 years when the comet finally returned, his predictions came true.

Sometimes, to figure out a problem, you have to take every bit of information and keep detailed records. You have to ask all the right questions. You have to follow every process to its end. This involves being very thorough.

> **"**Do not be desirous of having things done quickly. Do not look at small advantages. Desire to have things done quickly prevents their being done thoroughly. Looking at small advantages prevents great affairs from being accomplished.**"**
> —Confucius, Philosopher

What's in It for Me?

Thorough people can reap many benefits. For example, they can

- Be successful at work where their detail-oriented approach solves problems.

- Help others by their example.

- Become trusted to take the time and effort to get the right result.

- Make discoveries or solve problems because they take the time to get things right.

Related Words to Explore

Here are some words related to the trait of being thorough and to its opposite:

- Methodical
- Careful
- Excellent
- High quality
- Systematic
- Painstaking

- Meticulous
- Persistent
- Detailed
- Exhaustive
- Shoddy
- Superficial

TOLERANT

Tolerant people are able to accept differences among others. They don't impose their beliefs on others. They don't dislike people for what they believe. Being tolerant means not judging people based on where they live, how they look, or what their customs are.

Do you think of yourself as a tolerant person?

What Does It Mean to Be Tolerant?

To be tolerant can mean many things. It means you are understanding and open-minded. You dismiss, put up with, or even appreciate differences among people. You don't let things get to you. For example, you may be able to tolerate noisy neighbors better than others. Toleration can mean you don't get upset at annoyances. Or it can mean that you embrace other people's ways of doing things.

At the root of being tolerant is often an understanding of our own shortcomings. We're all only human. Our beliefs aren't necessarily better than other people's. They are just different. Tolerant people admit that their beliefs aren't the only beliefs.

Have you been tolerant of others? Can you enjoy people who are different without judging them? You may be a tolerant person.

Tolerance through Time

There have been many examples of tolerance in history. Here are a few:

- Freedom of religion has been part of American life since Europeans began arriving here. Many were running away from people who wouldn't let them follow their religious beliefs in their own countries. Freedom of religion means that you can practice the religion of your choice, or you can choose not to have a religion at all. Though various churches have had strong control over certain countries in history, in America no church is in control. Of course, individuals sometimes are intolerant of others in America, but the United States is set up to tolerate a variety of beliefs.

- Moving from one country to another is called immigration. America has been called the melting pot because, except for Native Americans, it is made up of immigrants from other countries and cultures. The history of immigration in America has not always been easy. Some groups have been intolerant of other groups. But today the various cultures have mixed together so much that we think of each other as Americans.

Sometimes people have difficulty appreciating different ways of doing things. They tolerate only their own ideas and customs. Learning to accept differences is a big part of tolerance, but sometimes that acceptance takes time. Is there somebody you know who is different from you? Could you get to know that person better and become more accepting of his or her differences?

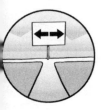

Being Tolerant in Life

Consider this situation:

> *Kendra was in charge of the decorations for the spring costume dance. She and her committee had decided people should wear costumes from the Wild West days of America, including cowboys, pioneer women, and Indians.*
>
> *After they announced their plan, John, a Native American, came to the principal to talk about it. The western expansion in America resulted in many Native Americans being killed. John didn't feel the school should make light of it. The principal told the committee the problem.*
>
> *Some kids started to say negative things about John. Kendra asked them to stop. She suggested they invite John to their next meeting and listen to his point of view. John came to their next meeting. He explained his concerns. Together with John, they came up with another idea for the party that was a great success.*

When somebody has a different point of view, it's easy to feel defensive. But it's often better to listen to his or her ideas and try to understand the person. Sometimes things done with the input of many people turn out better than those done with a single point of view.

> **"**What is toleration? It is the prerogative of humanity. We are all steeped in weaknesses and errors: Let us forgive one another's follies, it is the first law of nature.**"**
> —**Voltaire, Writer and Philosopher**

Being Tolerant in Practice

Pay attention to the people around you. Notice how their differences make them interesting. Think about how boring life would be if we were alike. Make a list of the differences between you and somebody else. Then list the similarities. No matter how much we are different, we are all people, so we have many things in common.

TOLERANCE CHECKLIST

○ Be open to learning about other people's beliefs and ideas.

○ Don't close your mind to new things.

○ Celebrate people's differences.

○ Understand that people have much in common.

○ Be eager to learn about other people so you can understand them better.

> **"**How far you go in life depends on your being tender with the young, compassionate with the aged, sympathetic with the striving, and tolerant of the weak and strong—because someday you will have been all of these.**"**
>
> —George Washington Carver, Former Slave, Educator, Scientist, Author

Tolerant Role Models

Here are people who have fought for the concept of tolerance.

- Paul Robeson was an All American football star at Rutgers University and was valedictorian of the class of 1918. He graduated from Columbia Law School at a time when it was very difficult for black people to succeed. He had a wonderful singing voice and became a star. During World War II, not one of the million black soldiers was awarded the Congressional Medal of Honor. These soldiers had separate facilities and transportation. Robeson fought against this prejudice. At the same time, he encouraged blacks to support the war effort so fascism could not "make slaves of us all." He used his fame to help the cause of tolerance and understanding among people.

- Derrick Bell has been a law professor and best-selling author. He was dismissed from Harvard Law School after a two-year leave of absence protesting the fact that Harvard employed few minority women on its faculty. He was a civil rights worker for the U.S. Justice Department and was asked to serve on the NAACP Legal Defense and Education Fund by Supreme Court Justice Thurgood Marshall. Though Bell describes himself as intolerant, he has worked for the idea that people shouldn't judge each other based on their differences. His book on the evils of racism is a standard at law schools.

What's in It for Me?

Consider these real-life consequences of being tolerant:

- You get to learn about other customs and ways of doing things.

- You don't prejudge people by their race, religion, or nationality, so you are exposed to new things.

- You are seen as kind and open-minded.

- You may get a job where your tolerance is helpful, such as a judge or social worker.

- You don't waste your time hating people for being different, so you accomplish more.

Related Words to Explore

Here are some words related to the trait of being tolerant and to its opposite:

- Broadminded
- Open-minded
- Liberal
- Understanding
- Compassionate

- Forbearing
- Lenient
- Intolerant
- Impatient
- Narrow-minded

TRUSTWORTHY

To be trustworthy simply means that people consider you to be worthy of their trust. You can be counted on to do what you say you'll do. You are somebody people trust not to tell a secret.

What do you do to earn other people's trust?

What Does It Mean to Be Trustworthy?

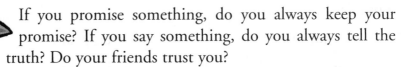

Has someone promised you something but then not come through? Do you still trust that person? People give trust to those who have a combination of the traits of dependability and honesty. Others trust what trustworthy people say because they don't lie and they follow through on what they say.

Trustworthy people are often given a great deal of responsibility because others know that they can count on them.

If you promise something, do you always keep your promise? If you say something, do you always tell the truth? Do your friends trust you?

Trustworthiness through Time

Here are examples from history of people trusting others:

- On D-day in World War II, the Allied forces from England, Canada, and the United States landed on the Normandy Coast in France. This huge attack on German troops turned the war around. Those making the plans had to trust each other to keep one of the most important secrets in history.

- Deep Throat was a code name given to a news source who provided information to two reporters about a break-in at the Democratic National Headquarters. The information Deep Throat provided to the reporters, Bob Woodward and Carl Bernstein, helped them reveal a cover-up that led to the resignation of President Richard Nixon. The reporters never revealed the name of Deep Throat, though they were pressured to. Finally, in 2005, Mark Felt, formerly with the F.B.I., admitted that he was Deep Throat. In more than 30 years, the reporters had never revealed his name. So that people will trust them with information, newspaper reporters promise not to reveal sources.

Often in our work, we are entrusted with information or secrets that we should not pass on. The success of an effort may depend on having people you trust working with you. Who do you trust most in the world? Why?

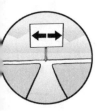

Being Trustworthy in Life

Consider this situation:

> *Jocelyn wanted to organize a surprise party for her friend Sara who was moving to another town. She needed somebody to help her with the arrangements. However, she worried that her friend Dana would talk about the party and ruin the surprise. Finally, she went to Jill and asked her if she would help with the party.*

> *Jill had a reputation for being trustworthy. She was a teacher's aide and had taken on a lot of responsibility. Whenever Jill promised to do something, she did it. Jill agreed to help Jocelyn with organizing the food and other details. She never said a word about the party. When Sara arrived at Jocelyn's house that Saturday, she was totally surprised.*

We all instinctively know which of our friends to trust with secrets and which we can depend on. Would you rather be somebody that people think they can trust or somebody who gets left out because you can't be trusted?

> **"**The only way to make a man trustworthy is to trust him.**"**
>
> **—Henry L. Stimson, Former Secretary of War**

Being Trustworthy in Practice

Do a survey of your friends. Ask them who they trust and why. Do most trust their family or friends? Do some trust teachers? What stories do they have about situations in which trust was broken? What did you learn that could help you become a more trustworthy person?

TRUSTWORTHINESS CHECKLIST

- ○ If you make a promise, keep it.
- ○ Always be honest with others.
- ○ Follow through when you say you will accomplish something.
- ○ Don't promise what you can't do.
- ○ If you disappoint somebody, make it up to him or her.

Trustworthy Role Models

These people have a reputation for being trustworthy.

- Colin L. Powell is a four-star general who has served in many positions of trust throughout his career. He served as Chairman of the Joint Chiefs of Staff for President George H. Bush. During that time, he helped lead the military to victory in the Persian Gulf War. In 2001, the U.S. Senate showed their trust in him by unanimously confirming him to become the first African American Secretary of State. He served as the Secretary of State for President George W. Bush during the first four years of his presidency. Although Colin Powell sometimes disagreed with decisions made by the presidents he served, they could trust him to work hard to carry out their policies.

- Alan Greenspan has been the Chairman of the Federal Reserve Board since 1987. His job is in part to increase public confidence in our economy. Several presidents have relied on his abilities to lead the way in improving areas such as inflation and unemployment. In 1998, consumer confidence in our economy hit a 30-year high. Though not all his choices have been correct, generally people trust him to use his power well to keep our country on an even course.

People who go into public service as politicians or government economists, for example, work hard to gain the trust of their citizens. In their cases, if they lose public trust, they will probably lose their jobs. How important is it for an employer to trust an employee? Will you be a trustworthy worker? Are you a trustworthy friend?

Young Person's Character Education Handbook, © JIST Life

What's in It for Me?

Consider these real-life consequences of being trustworthy:

- Employers may give you great responsibility and promotions.

- You are viewed as somebody who gets the job done.

- People will open up to you about their lives because they trust you not to tell their secrets.

- You feel a sense of accomplishment when you do what you promised to do.

Related Words to Explore

Here are some words related to the trait of being trustworthy and to its opposite:

- Dependable
- Reliable
- Responsible
- Truthful
- Honest

- Constant
- Honorable
- Untrustworthy
- Corrupt

VISIONARY

When you look up the definition of *visionary*, you see words like *creativity* and *imagination*. How is a visionary person different from a creative person? A visionary person is not only creative, but that person dreams of something totally new, something that has never been done before. An artist can be creative but is not always visionary. You may come up with a creative solution to a problem, but it may not differ dramatically from other solutions.

Do you have it in you to be visionary?

What Does It Mean to Be Visionary?

A visionary person is also sometimes referred to as one who sees things others can't see. A vision itself can be a dream, a delusion, or just a new idea nobody has ever thought of before.

Visionary people usually combine this trait with some talent or interest to focus their vision. For example, a visionary musician might write a new type of music. A visionary architect might build new types of buildings. A visionary scientist might come up with a cure for a disease or a new way of thinking about the universe.

Sometimes visionary people come up with ideas but not the method of putting them into practice. They might rely on others to build the machines they imagine, prove the theories they come up with, or play the music they write.

   Young Person's Character Education Handbook, © JIST Life

Visionaries through Time

In science, being visionary is a way of life. Scientists question the current thinking or try to prove new theories. But what scientific breakthroughs have been truly visionary?

- Nanotechnology is the science of anything small—really small. Nanotechnology deals with things at the level of molecules and atoms. When you work at this tiny level, you can make stronger materials, deliver drugs with no side effects, and create treatments to fight cancer. Nanotechnology is the result of several visionary people's efforts. These people had to imagine a world too small to see and wonder about its properties. They had to create new ways to measure these properties because they couldn't see or touch the materials they created. They had to find ways to build things in the way that they are built in nature, molecule by molecule.

- At one time, doctors had very little idea of what makes us sick. They didn't understand how germs worked, traveling from one person to another. They didn't know how the blood circulated in the body. Many people had to make great leaps in imagining what goes on inside our bodies when we get sick. People such as Robert Boyle, Robert Hooke, and Louis Pasteur, who created the germ theory, had to make great leaps to figure out how disease and our bodies work.

Can you look at a blade of grass and imagine how it lives, takes in nourishment, and grows? Do you wonder what it would be like to encounter alien races? Can you imagine the future from the present? If so, you may have visionary talent!

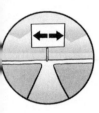

Being Visionary in Life

Consider this situation:

When Ms. Woodrow announced the theme of the final project for the year, Elana's mind started working. Students were to do a report on the life and work of an American author. The format of the report was wide open.

Elana approached Ms. Woodrow with a few questions. Could I give my report somewhere else in the school? Could I use music and drama? Ms. Woodrow was hesitant to have Elana give the report outside the classroom because nobody had ever done that. But she agreed.

Elana spent a lot of time preparing for her presentation. She got a few friends to help. Marc was an audio-visual expert who did special effects for school plays. Maria loved music and would help pick out the perfect music.

Before the presentation Elana was nervous. Ms. Woodrow agreed to lead the students onto the darkened auditorium stage. The curtain was closed, and mysterious music played. A flickering candle lighted the space as Elana entered, sat on a stool, and began to read an Edgar Allen Poe story. At the most dramatic moment in the story, she stopped, the lights came up, and Elana began her report about Poe.

Elana wanted to create a completely different setting for a school report. How was Elana visionary in trying something new? What grade do you think she received?

   Young Person's Character Education Handbook, © JIST Life

Being Visionary in Practice

Look at something in your life from a new angle. If your family fights over which video to rent Friday night, can you come up with a totally new way to make that choice? If you can't figure out how to complete a science fair project, could you do something nobody has done before? Try sitting with a friend and brainstorming completely new ways of approaching things. You might be surprised at what you come up with when you ignore what's in place today and focus on tomorrow.

VISIONARY CHECKLIST

- ⬭ Don't let yourself be limited by the way things have always been done.
- ⬭ Ask yourself, "What if?"
- ⬭ Look at things in an entirely new way.
- ⬭ Get excited by possibilities.
- ⬭ Learn from history, but don't be bound by it.

> **❝** *Imagination is more important than knowledge.* **❞**
> —**Albert Einstein**

Visionary Role Models

Here are some people who have a reputation for being visionary:

- H.G. Wells was born in 1866 in England. He became one of the first science fiction writers in the world. His books, *The Time Machine, The War of the Worlds*, and *The Invisible Man,* are classics. He explored ideas about alien races, time travel, and futuristic scientific advances. He made surprisingly accurate predictions about space flight.

- Leonardo da Vinci was a man of many talents. He was an accomplished painter. He was an inventor who made drawings for devices such as the helicopter, parachute, and armored vehicle, all in the 1400s! He had a fascination with machines that allowed him to break down their various parts and imagine new machines, which few people of his day did.

- Frank Lloyd Wright was a visionary architect. Before him, houses were box-like, with many small, separate rooms. Wright pioneered the idea of open floor plans, where one room flows into the other. He created an organic style of design, where a house fits in with its surroundings. Wright imagined and built a new style of American housing.

Visionaries are people who don't just imagine new ideas or a different future. These people act on their visions. They create literature, buildings, or machines that change our lives. Can you think of other visionary people who changed the world with their ideas?

Young Person's Character Education Handbook, © JIST Life

What's in It for Me?

Visionary people can have a difficult time because they have to convince others to look at things differently. Many people resist that kind of change. However, successful visionary people can reap many benefits. These people can

- Have great financial success and even fame for being the first to envision something.

- Contribute to positive change in our society.

- Help establish new movements, industries, or products that grow from their vision.

- Get interesting jobs where they can use their creativity and imaginations every day.

Related Words to Explore

Here are some words related to the trait of being visionary and to its opposite:

- Farsighted
- Imaginative
- Creative
- Focused
- Idealistic

- Narrowly focused
- Small-minded
- Unimaginative
- Limited

WISE

Being wise doesn't mean being smart. Wise people have good sense and show good judgment. They learn from their experiences, so they know more than just facts. They learn about people and human nature. They learn what works and what doesn't.

Do you consider yourself a person with good sense?

What Does It Mean to Be Wise?

If you make the same mistakes again and again, you won't be thought of as wise. On the other hand, if you learn from mistakes and think things through carefully before acting, you may be wise.

Wise people don't act without thinking or act out of pure emotion. They observe the world around them. Then they act in ways that make sense based on those observations.

Although people may be smart, they are wise only if they use their intelligence to act with good sense based on experience. How many wise people do you know?

Young Person's Character Education Handbook, © JIST Life

Wisdom through Time

There are examples of groups that are considered wise.

- The Seven Wise Men of Greece were a group of people who tried to acquire wisdom. They established the first school of Greek philosophy. They were known in their own time as *sages*, which means, "those who know." Later, they were called *philosophers*. Philosophers are people who use their knowledge and love of truth to become wiser. Different philosophers believe different things. What they have in common is a desire to understand the world around them.

- Wizards, such as Merlin of King Arthur's court, are found often in fable and literature. They may be based on wise men found in various cultures. Among various cultures, the wise person of a tribe or group may be called by other names, such as a *shaman*, *medicine man*, or *mystic*. People look to these individuals for guidance and advice.

Becoming wise is not easy. It takes a lot of experience and learning to be wise. Those who want to develop their common sense and judgment and learn the truth may develop wisdom.

> **"**All receive advice. Only the wise profit from it.**"**
> —**Pubilius Syrus, Roman Philosopher**

Being Wise in Life

Consider this situation:

> *Ms. Torvald had been the guidance counselor at Franklin Middle School for two years. One day, the parents of twins Alan and Scott came to see her. They were frustrated because, though Alan was an excellent student, Scott was having problems with a few courses.*

> *"Alan comes home and does his homework without us asking," said their father. "We have to force Scott to sit down, and then he doesn't pay attention to his work." Over the past week, Ms. Torvald had observed Scott and Alan and talked to their teachers, knowing this meeting was coming up.*

> *She pointed out that Scott was more interested in sports and activities than Alan. Forcing him to sit still after a long day of schoolwork was perhaps not the right thing to do. "Alan is more studious. Homework comes naturally to him. But why don't you let Scott go out and play for an hour or so before doing his homework. You might find he can focus better. Even though the boys are twins, you can't treat them the same."*

Ms. Torvald took time to observe these two boys and draw some wise conclusions. Sometimes we treat everybody the same when it would be wiser to observe people and learn from their differences.

Being Wise in Practice

Pick a philosopher such as Aristotle, Socrates, or Immanuel Kant and study his philosophy. What conclusions did that person draw about life and people? What kind of observations did he make? Do you think they are true today? Because the world changes, our observations about it may change over time, too.

WISDOM CHECKLIST

○ Observe the world around you, and learn from it.

○ Try to think things through carefully.

○ Don't act from your emotions, but use your experiences to guide your actions.

○ Understand that wisdom isn't something you acquire overnight.

○ Learn from what wise people around you and in history have said and done.

Wise Role Models

Here are people with a reputation for being wise.

- Helen Keller, described in the "adaptable" section, was more challenged than most to observe the world and learn from it. When she was two, she got sick and as a result became blind and deaf. With the help of others, she learned to communicate and read books in Braille format. She wrote books that helped others to understand the experience of the disabled. Helen Keller grew wise from her experiences and gave us insight into how to overcome challenges in our life.

- Jurgen Habermas is a German philosopher. He is often called a sage who has commented about many of the problems of modern life. Habermas is a practical person who has applied his experience to a discussion of how people of different cultures can better communicate and come to agreement.

Throughout time, wise people have often communicated their conclusions about the world. Whether they are writers, philosophers, or from some other field, their words are useful to us. Take the time to read works by people who are considered wise. That may help you become wise yourself.

Young Person's Character Education Handbook, © JIST Life

What's in It for Me?

Consider these real-life consequences of being wise:

- Others look to you for advice and guidance.

- At work, you are respected and looked up to.

- You act with good sense and judgment.

- You continue to learn from things and people around you throughout your whole life.

Related Words to Explore

Here are some words related to the trait of being wise and to its opposite:

- Shrewd
- Intelligent
- Astute
- Clever
- Prudent

- Sensible
- Judicious
- Foolish
- Silly

MORE CHARACTER EDUCATION RESOURCES

This section describes Web sites, other books, and videos that will help you learn more about character.

Web Sites

- Athletes for a Better World (ABW) uses sports to develop character, teamwork, and citizenship. **www.aforbw.org**

- CHARACTER COUNTS! teaches the "six pillars of character": trustworthiness, respect, responsibility, fairness, caring, and citizenship. **www.charactercounts.org**

- Do Something gives you ideas and inspiration to make change possible. **www.dosomething.org**

- The Foundation for a Better Life site provides stories that communicate the values that make a difference in our communities. **www.forbetterlife.org**

- HumanityQuest.com explores more than 500 human values, using online study groups, discussions groups, creative arts activities, and computer technology. **http://humanityquest.com**

- The Josephson Institute of Ethics's quote library inspires you to make good choices. **www.josephsoninstitute.org/quotes/quotetoc.htm**

- TIME profiles 100 people who have influenced the world during the past 100 years. **www.time.com/time/time100**

- The Wisdom Quotes site is a collection of quotes designed to inspire and challenge you. Search the quote database containing hundreds of topics. **www.wisdomquotes.com**

- Youth Activism aims to prove that you can play a major role in positive change. **www.youthactivism.com**

Books

- *Character Education Activities.* A workbook that emphasizes the importance of honesty, respect, courage, and other traits. Includes 147 activities, worksheets, and checklists.

- *Character: A Guide for Middle Grade Students.* This workbook helps you think about who you are and the character traits to develop. Includes examples, activities, and exercises.

The books are available at www.jist.com or by calling 1-800-648-JIST.

Videos

Exploring Your Character. This informational video shows how to believe in yourself and make a difference in others' lives.

A separate video is available for school administrators and teachers.

The videos are available at www.jist.com or by calling 1-800-648-JIST.

To Teachers, Counselors, and Other Adults

JIST Life offers a complete line of helpful and interesting character education resources. Please call 1-800-648-JIST for a catalog and more information.

A

abrasive, 135
abstemious, 249
accommodating, 15, 63, 273
accountable, 4-9, 237
active, 141
adaptable, 10-15
adjustable, 15
adventurous, 33, 69
affirmative, 219
afraid, 69
alert, 117
altruistic, 16-21
ambitious, 22-27
answerable, 9, 237
apathetic, 141, 177
arrogant, 165
artistic, 75
assiduous, 147
astute, 303
autonomous, 255
aware, 267

B-C

biased, 111
bighearted, 129
boastful, 165
bold, 28-33, 69
boss, 189
brave, 33, 69
broadminded, 285

callous, 267
calm, 135
capable, 147, 225
careful, 45, 279
caring, 21, 34-39, 51, 57, 135
cautious, 40-45
certain, 81
changeable, 15, 99
cheerful, 183
chief, 189
civil, 213

classy, 105
clear thinking, 81
clever, 225, 303
cold, 39
collaborative, 273
comic, 261
committed, 87
common, 171
compassionate, 39, 46-51, 285
concentrating, 117
concerned, 21, 39, 45, 51
conforming, 15
considerate, 52-57, 231
constant, 195, 291
constructive, 219
contentious, 63
cooperative, 58-63, 153, 273
corrupt, 291
couch potato, 147
courageous, 64-69
courteous, 213
crass, 105
creative, 70-75, 297
critical, 219
cruel, 51
curious, 177

D

dangerous, 45
deceptive, 159
decisive, 33, 76-81
decorous, 105
dedicated, 82-87, 99, 195
deferential, 231
definite, 33
dependable, 88-93, 159, 237, 291
dependent, 225, 255
detailed, 279
determined, 27, 81, 94-99, 117
devoted, 87, 195
dignified, 100-105
diligent, 147
direct, 9
director, 189

irresolute, 99
isolated, 273

J-L

jesting, 261
joking, 261
joyful, 178-183
judicious, 303
just, 111

kind, 21, 39, 57, 135
kindhearted, 51

lazy, 27, 147, 249
leader, 184-189
lenient, 123, 285
lethargic, 183
liable, 9, 237
liberal, 129, 201, 285
limited, 297
lively, 183
loner, 63
loving, 39
loyal, 87, 93, 190-195

M-N

magnanimous, 123
manager, 189
meek, 165
merciful, 123
methodical, 279
meticulous, 279
mild, 135
moderate, 45, 249
modern, 171
modest, 165
motivated, 27
munificent, 129

narrowly focused, 297
narrow-minded, 201, 285
nationalistic, 141
needy, 255
negative, 219
noble, 105
nondiscriminatory, 111

nosy, 177
nurturing, 39

O-P

obliging, 63, 153
obnoxious, 213
obstructive, 153
open-minded, 196-201, 285
opinionated, 33
optimistic, 183, 219
original, 75, 171
outspoken, 33
owning up to, 9

painstaking, 279
pardoning, 123
passive, 141
patient, 45, 202-207
paying attention, 117
peaceful, 135
perceptive, 267
persistent, 207, 279
pessimistic, 183, 219
philanthropic, 129
pioneering, 171
poised, 243
polite, 57, 208-213, 231
positive, 81, 183, 214-219
prejudiced, 201
probing, 177
prudent, 303
prying, 177

Q-R

questioning, 177

rational, 111
ready to lend a hand, 153
reasonable, 111
reckless, 45
redundant, 171
refined, 93, 195, 213
reliable, 93, 237, 291
reserved, 33, 183, 243
resolute, 81, 93, 99
resourceful, 220-225

V-Z

Young Person's Occupational Outlook Handbook

Based on the U.S. Department of Labor's *Occupational Outlook Handbook,* this guidebook is ideal for helping middle-school children explore careers through an interesting format. It groups together related job descriptions, making it easy to study job options based on interests. The text stresses the connection between school subjects and jobs and gives essential facts for evaluating and exploring careers of interest.

The descriptions cover more than 270 jobs held by 88 percent of the U.S. workforce. Each one-page overview includes the following:

○ Brief description of the job

○ School subjects related to the job

○ At-a-glance facts on education, earnings, and job outlook

⌒ n activities for "trying out" the job

⌒ other occupations related to each job

⌒ g tidbits about the job's history and

$19.95

1-59357-125-9

de LP-J1259

313

Index J0-648-JIST or visit www.jist.com